DOMESTIC

P9-CBT-033

ESSAYS ON INFLATION AND INDEXATION

Herbert Giersch • Milton Friedman
William Fellner • Edward M. Bernstein
Alexandre Kafka

ESSAYS ON INFLATION
AND INDEXATION

ESSAYS ON INFLATION
AND INDEXATION

Herbert Giersch • Milton Friedman
William Fellner • Edward M. Bernstein
Alexandre Kafka

American Enterprise Institute for Public Policy Research
Washington, D. C.

HERBERT GIERSCH is director of the Institute for World Economics at the University of Kiel in West Germany.

MILTON FRIEDMAN is Paul Snowden Russell distinguished service professor of economics at the University of Chicago.

WILLIAM FELLNER is a member of the President's Council of Economic Advisers and Sterling professor of economics, emeritus, at Yale University.

EDWARD M. BERNSTEIN is chairman of the board of EMB, Ltd., a private economic research group in Washington, D. C.

ALEXANDRE KAFKA is executive director of the International Monetary Fund and professor of economics at the University of Virginia.

ISBN 0-8447-3139-0

Domestic Affairs Study 24, October 1974

Library of Congress Catalog Card No. 74-18963

Printed in the United States of America

CONTENTS

1
INDEX CLAUSES AND THE FIGHT AGAINST INFLATION

Herbert Giersch

With an appendix by Adolf Ahnefeld and K.-H. Frank
Translated by Eric Schiff

1. Economic growth proceeds in business cycles extending over several years. From cycle to cycle the value of money has shrunk more and more during the last ten to fifteen years. At the end of the present cycle, there will probably be a decline in the rate of price increase, especially if stability continues to be the aim of demand management. But there is reason to expect that this decline will again be only temporary. For, unless we have some new ideas, it will be impossible to apply the brakes to inflation without causing some loss of employment. As soon as the rate of unemployment is. clearly rising again, the need for another "leap forward" will be felt too keenly for policy makers to resist. The business cycle that will then begin will bring a renewed acceleration of inflation, and so on. This, at any rate, is what things look like if the past trend of inflation is projected into the future.

2. Past experiences leave their imprint on expectations. If the rates of price increase abate in the near future, many people will undoubtedly feel reassured and will no longer be thinking of the overall trend. But it is equally certain that the accelerated pace of

The author's thanks for numerous suggestions go primarily to Hans Möller, Munich, Alfred Müller-Armack, Cologne, Otto Pfleiderer, Stuttgart, and Hans Willgerodt, Cologne, for the detailed comments they have offered on earlier drafts. Grateful acknowledgment for such suggestions is also due to the author's collaborators at the Institut für Weltwirtschaft, in particular to Adolf Ahnefeld, Hubertus Müller-Groeling, Klaus-Dieter Schmidt, and Peter Trapp. In the work on the latest version, I was greatly helped by continuous discussions with Roland Vaubel. Of course, none of the persons named is in any way responsible for such mistakes and shortcomings as may still be in the text.

This paper was originally published as Kiel Discussion Paper No. 32, Institut für Weltwirtschaft, Kiel, October 1973; it was revised by the author for the English edition.

inflation in the subsequent boom will be a source of disappointment, giving rise to an even more intense pessimism. Reflecting this state of mind, interest rates, real estate prices, and wage increases will contain higher inflation components. This adjustment will probably take place much more swiftly in the future than it did in the past. People have learned how to live with inflation; they have become used to it. To the extent that the experience of inflation gives rise to expectations of future inflation which are then built into the prices, wages, and interest rates agreed upon for the future, it becomes itself an element of cost inflation, and thereby a driving force in the inflationary process. Those who have hedged against inflation by acquiring real assets or by incurring huge debts will soon cease to be enemies of inflation. And those who anticipate the full extent of a prospective inflation, who are able to conclude collective wage agreements for relatively short terms or who know that wildcat strikes will not be persecuted, will no longer consider the fight against inflation to be a matter of particular importance. Moreover, when the population has grown accustomed to inflation, restoration of monetary stability becomes more difficult, more time consuming and, possibly, more painful. At least this holds so long as our economic policy lacks new inspiration.

The classical prescription for curing the economy of the habit-forming drug of inflation is clear: The only way to achieve a gradual stabilization of the value of money without causing any substantive decline in employment is to eliminate, everywhere and simultaneously, the expectation of inflation by lowering, step by step and in a manner avoiding frictions, the rate of growth in the money supply and in wage increases—which in due course would also permit a reduction in interest rates. In 1965, such a program was advocated by the German Council of Economic Experts as "concerted action" with a view to avoiding a stabilization crisis (such as we actually did get afterwards). But such a program would presumably be rejected today as it was then—all the more so since, in the meantime, the task has become more difficult and the sociopolitical climate has grown colder. At the same time, just as in the earlier instance, a decrease in employment would be considered too high a price to pay for monetary stability. What path can lead us out of this blind alley?

3. A program attacking the problem of prices directly, that is, by a price freeze, would presumably be popular because it would seem to hold out the prospect of a radical cure. To be sure, in the Federal Republic as in other countries, there are also economists who *would* advocate it. There exists, after all, a doctrine—one that com-

mands and deserves attention—which makes direct intervention in product and factor prices appear to be a viable solution. With respect to the question of what determines the price level in an economy that is either virtually closed or has a floating currency, two schools of thought stand in opposition to each other. The "monetarists," reasoning along the lines of the old Currency Theory, read the famous quantity equation of exchange [1] from left to right, implying that (assuming the velocity of circulation as given) the quantity of money determines the price level of commodities and services traded (the national product). The other group, which may be considered Keynesian, reasons the other way. With Joan Robinson—and approximately in accord with the Banking Theory—this group holds that the volume of transactions and the price level are determined exogenously, thus representing data to which the volume of money and its velocity of circulation adjust themselves.[2] Now, if it is believed that the price level is a political phenomenon,[3] the idea of subjecting it to control by political agencies is not far-fetched. John Kenneth Galbraith and all those economists who applauded Nixon on 15 August 1971 have drawn this inference—it being obvious by then that incomes policy as a milder form of controlling the price level had not worked well.

4. By contrast, the monetarists have no sympathy for price freezes. They stress the importance of controlling the quantity of money. The inflation which is in store for us is, according to them, programmed in advance by the development of the money supply.

> On the average, a change in the rate of monetary growth produces a change in the rate of growth of nominal income about six or nine months later. . . . On the average, the effect on prices comes about six to nine months after the effect on income and output, so the total delay between a change in monetary growth and a change in the rate of inflation averages something like 12-18 months.[4]

---

[1] $MV = PQ$, where M = volume of money, V = velocity of circulation of money, P = average price level, and Q = quantity of output traded.

[2] On this contradistinction of views, see Joan Robinson, "Quantity Theories, Old and New," *Journal of Money, Credit, and Banking*, vol. 2 (1970), p. 504ff.

[3] Joan Robinson writes: "The main moral of the General Theory can be expressed by saying that the general price level in terms of money is not a monetary phenomenon; its movement depends mainly on money-wage bargains; that is to say, it is very largely a political phenomenon." Ibid., p. 512.

[4] M. Friedman, "The Counter-Revolution in Monetary Theory," First Wincott Memorial Lecture, Occasional Paper 33 (London: Institute of Economic Affairs, 1970), p. 22ff.

It is true that one cannot determine in advance the precise rate of monetary expansion which monetary policy must aim at in order to achieve stability in the value of money. But it can be said that the rate lies in the neighborhood of the rate at which the productive potential of the economy as a whole is growing. In the process of stabilization it is impossible to make sure that physical quantities will not respond in a manner entailing some reduction in employment. But these effects can be mitigated by a policy under which the process of bringing the rate of monetary expansion down to the level of the "stability rate" moves only gradually.

To avoid major repercussions in physical quantities, it is also necessary that people keep their price and income demands flexible. These demands should be based not on inflation rates of the past, but rather on those lower future inflation rates which monetary policy will tolerate. This is exactly what will be achieved by concluding agreements containing cost-of-living escalator clauses.

5. Escalator clauses of one form or other have, in fact, been advocated by monetarists (for example, Milton Friedman) and by their precursors (for example, Irving Fisher), as well as by Edgeworth, Marshall, the earlier Keynes (1927), Musgrave, Machlup, Palander, Slichter, Tobin, and, in the German-speaking countries, by Jöhr, Pfleiderer, Stucken, and Timm.[5]

---

[5] M. Friedman, *An Economist's Protest: Columns in Political Economy* (Glen Ridge, N. J., 1972), p. 84ff.; M. Friedman and F. Machlup, in "Monetary Policy and the Management of the Public Debt: Their Role in Achieving Price Stability and High-Level Employment," U.S. Congress, Joint Committee on the Economic Report, Replies to Questions and Other Material for Use of the Subcommittee on General Credit Control and Debt Management, 82d Congress, 2d session (1952), p. 1105ff.; for the reference to S. H. Slichter, see ibid., p. 1111ff.; Irving Fisher, assisted by H. R. Cohrssen, *Stable Money: A History of the Movement* (New York, 1934), p. 112; I. Fisher, assisted by H. G. Brown, *The Purchasing Power of Money, Its Determination and Relation to Credit, Interest, and Crises* (New York, 1911); W. S. Jevons, *Money and the Mechanism of Exchange* (London, 1875), p. 332ff.; F. Y. Edgeworth, *Papers Relating to Political Economy* (London, 1925), vol. 1, section 3; A. Marshall, *Money, Credit and Commerce* (London, 1923), p. 36ff.; Marshall, "Answer to Questions on the Subject of Currency and Prices," *Third Report of the Royal Commission Appointed to Inquire into the Depression of Trade and Industry* (London, 1886), p. 423, in Marshall, *Official Papers* (London, 1926), p. 10ff.; Marshall, "Remedies for Fluctuations of General Prices," *The Contemporary Review*, March 1887, in *Memorials of Alfred Marshall*, ed. A. C. Pigou (New York, 1956), p. 188ff.; J. M. Keynes, statement before the Committee on National Debt and Taxation (Colwyn Committee), *Minutes of Evidence* (London, 1927), vol. 1, p. 278ff.; Keynes, "The Colwyn Report on National Debt and Taxation," *The Economic Journal* (London), vol. 37 (1927), p. 211ff.; Keynes, "The Prospects of Money," *The Economic Journal*, vol. 24 (1914), p. 610ff.; Keynes, "Review of Fisher's 'Purchasing Power of Money,'" *The Economic Journal*, vol. 21 (1911), p. 393ff.; G. L. Bach and R. A. Musgrave, "A Stable Purchasing Power Bond," *The Ameri-*

6. On the other hand, there is the widespread opinion that index clauses accelerate the inflationary process. Those who start from the assumption that the level of wages and prices is determined historically and politically must be inclined to hold this view. But the view also depends on the further assumption that a monetary inflation potential exists:

—either because—as is typical at the beginning of an inflation—an unanticipated monetary expansion has taken place, creating an excess supply of money;

—or because the central bank, for reasons of external economic policy, is not in a position to limit the volume of money effectively (for example, when, under free convertibility and fixed exchange rates, the currency of the country is undervalued), which means that the supply of money is very elastic.

In these cases, the price increase is not limited by anything that happens on the money side, but only by frictions and lagged responses ("inertia"), or by moral suasion vis-à-vis various social groups and institutions—those engaged in collective wage bargaining, suppliers of goods or services, and government officials. The price rise may also be limited by expectations which only incompletely anticipate an impending shrinkage of the value of money (the "money illusion"), with the result that inflation-caused losses arise. Under such circumstances the inflationary process would indeed be accelerated if important brakes were loosened, say, by permitting—let alone advocating—escalator clauses in collective wage agreements.

can Economic Review, vol. 31 (1941), p. 823ff.; T. Palander, Värdebeständighet: Ett problem vid sparande, livförsäkringar och pensioner (Stockholm, 1957); J. Tobin, "An Essay on Principles of Debt Management," in Fiscal and Debt Management Policies, a series of research studies prepared for the Commission on Money and Credit (Englewood Cliffs, N. J., 1963), p. 202ff.; W. A. Jöhr, "Inflationsbekämpfung und Indexierung," comments on H. Sieber, "Lösung des Inflationsproblems durch Indexierung," Wirtschaft und Recht (Zurich), vol. 19 (1967), p. 33ff.; O. Pfleiderer, "Berücksichtigung der Geldentwertung bei der Besteuerung von Zinserträgen?" Zeitschrift für das gesamte Kreditwesen (Frankfurt), vol. 18 (1965), p. 886ff.; Pfleiderer, "Zur Frage der Zulassung von Wertbeständigkeitsklauseln im langfristigen Kapitalverkehr" (unpublished manuscript); R. Stucken, "Die wertbeständigen Anleihen in finanzwirtschaftlicher Betrachtung," Schriften des Vereins für Socialpolitik (Munich, Leipzig), 1924; Stucken, Was stimmt nicht mit unserem Geld? (Hamburg, 1967), p. 82ff.; H. Timm, "Der Einfluss von Geldwertsicherungsklauseln auf Geldkapitalangebot und -nachfrage und auf die schleichende Inflation," Jahrbuch für Nationalökonomie und Statistik (Stuttgart), vol. 180 (1967), p. 313ff.; "Geldwertsicherungsklauseln in der schleichenden Inflation," Wirtschaftsdienst (Hamburg), vol. 52 (1972), p. 641ff.

7. However, what we are having at present is a fully developed inflation, not an incipient one. Nor has much of the money illusion remained with us. Besides, ever since flexible exchange rates and swift adjustments of parity values have become the general practice, we have seen that the central bank is fully able to apply the monetary brakes. So let us assume that the central bank uses the means at its disposal to reduce the rate of monetary growth to a level compatible with stability.

If escalator provisions are forbidden and not in use, there is a strong tendency to build the inflation rate of the past into the new collective agreements, especially in those cases where no loss in employment has occurred as yet. For example, if a 4 percent rise in productivity is in prospect, and if the rate of inflation in the recent past was 8 percent, then wage increases to the tune of 12 percent will have to be expected. (All figures represent annual rates.) Now if the central bank succeeds, by a restrictive credit policy, in reducing the price increase from 8 percent to 5 percent, the rise in real wages will not be 4 percent but 7 percent, far exceeding what would be in line with the growth of productivity. This would entail a marked decline in employment, a typical stabilization crisis which, by all experience, would very soon lead to a resumption of the expansionist policy.

By contrast, if wage contracts with escalator clauses are permitted and are in use, the reduction in the rate of inflation will not result in unintended rises in real wages that would bring about losses in employment. This is so because in this case collective bargaining agreements provide for a rise in real wages at a specified rate, namely, the rate that conforms to the rise in productivity—let us again say 4 percent—and for a variable inflation adjustment determined ex post in conformity with the inflation that actually took place. No matter how high or low the inflation rate, real wages rise 4 percent, neither more nor less. If the rate of inflation can be brought down from 8 percent to 5 percent, nominal wages will not rise by 12 percent but only by 9 percent. If it proves feasible to reduce the inflation rate to zero, nominal wages will be only 4 percent higher, and so stabilization policy will not send up real wages by more than that rate. Hence, if wages are tied to a cost-of-living index, the risk of a decline in employment is minimized. Wages with escalator provisions are flexible wages. They, and only they, open the way to a prompt and consistent stabilization without any stabilization crisis and without wage control. If the escalator clause operates symmetrically, that is, downward as well as upward, then even an outright decrease in the price level will not result in any loss of employment.

8. Escalator clauses in capital transactions have similar effects. For example, with escalator provisions in loan contracts, creditor-debtor relations are "as if" the value of money were still (or again) stable.[6] In lieu of a fixed nominal interest rate of, say, 11 percent, consisting of a "real" rate (3 percent) and an inflation rate (8 percent) that has been assumed ex ante, only the "real" interest rate is settled as a fixed component. The nominal interest payments, as well as the amount representing capital repayment, vary automatically (ex post) with the actual rate of inflation. If the inflation was correctly antici-pated by the contracting parties, loans with escalator provisions will neither benefit nor harm anybody. If the prospective rate of inflation has been generally underestimated, escalator clauses prevent an inflation-caused gain from accruing to the debtor; they protect in this case creditors and savers. It is true that the number of people inclined to combat inflation would thereby decrease, but so would the number of those interested in the continuation or acceleration of the infla-tionary process. If the inflation is being slowed down, contrary to the interests of those who incurred debts carrying high interest rates, then those debtors whose loans have escalator clauses will not be disap-pointed, nor will they undergo any crisis caused by an excessive debt burden. Those who have financed their investments by credit con-tracts under which the "real" interest rates do not go up when the actual inflation rate stays below the expected one need not be afraid of stabilization. At the time they made the investments, it was already necessary for them to figure things out "as if" the value of money were stable. For these reasons, loans with escalator provisions, besides protecting creditors and savers, provide protection from a stabilization crisis. Therefore, such loans should not only be permitted; they should also be encouraged by all means.

9. Furthermore, loans carrying escalator clauses help to avoid or to reduce those distortions in the structure of production and prices that originate in an inflation-caused flight from money into real assets. Under inflation, money loses its ability to function as a store of value. This makes investors, fearing further shrinkage of money value, turn to gold, real estate, houses, and condominium apartments. If the supply of these assets is elastic, real productive forces are being channeled into such "concrete gold." Loans with escalator clauses do

---

[6] What is being agreed upon is a repayment exceeding the original loan by the percentage by which the price index—say, the cost-of-living index—has risen by the time of repayment. A further point of the agreement provides for a "real" interest rate, which means that the annual or semiannual interest payments, like the sum representing repayment, will rise in proportion to the shrinkage in money value that has taken place in the meantime.

preserve real values; they are therefore an effective device for preventing an inflation-induced building boom and an updrift of real estate prices that otherwise would be unavoidable under high and rising expectations for further inflation.

The sooner we introduce loans with escalator clauses, and the wider they spread, the less reason there will be to expect that stabilization will cause a breakdown in the construction sector, and the easier it will be, therefore, to return to monetary stability.

10. A number of arguments against escalator clauses have been raised in the literature and must be discussed here. For the sake of completeness we first mention a few objections that can be dealt with briefly.

(a) It is objected that escalator provisions do not, in inflation, provide any protection for holders of cash. This is of course true, but would be an objection only if someone said that such provisions are a panacea.

(b) It is argued that escalator provisions are to the disadvantage of the weaker market parties because, unlike the more powerful parties, they cannot secure acceptance of these provisions. This argument overlooks the following: The more powerful parties use their opportunities anyway, regardless of whether there are escalator clauses or not. Indeed, one might well think that if escalator provisions were forbidden, the weaker market parties, which by all experience are the ones that have to have the strongest apprehensions regarding the risk connected with inflation, would be deprived right at the outset (by the law itself) of an important chance to hedge against the unpleasant consequences of inflation.

(c) Mention is sometimes made of the possibility that the government, at some future time, might go back on its promise to insure the real value of the government securities in the hands of the public, or that it might even forbid, retroactively, the use of escalator clauses in private contracts. This apprehension is based on experiences under governments that cannot be compared with a government under which the rule of law is established, as it is in the Federal Republic.

(d) The fear is sometimes voiced that the government might manipulate the price index. In the light of some isolated events abroad, this fear is perhaps not without foundation. But in the Federal Republic, with its independent statistical agencies, the situation is, after all, quite different. Besides, an alert and watchful community is nowadays so informed about matters of economic policy that the risk of manipulation can be kept within narrow limits. As a debtor in loans with escalator clauses, the government may be interested in manipulating the index downward. But this cannot possibly be justified as an act of self-defense—all the less so since the real revenue from taxes rises with the inflation (unless the tax rates themselves are pegged to an index). For the rest, should the government as a debtor owing loans with escalator clauses try to tamper with the price index, it would jeopardize its credit rating for a long time to come.

The objection that any index measures the shrinkage in money value only incompletely carries little weight: an inadequate index is always better than no index at all.

(e) It has been argued that loans having escalator provisions leave debtors in the dark about the actual cost of the loan, thereby making exact calculation more difficult for them. This objection, however, is couched in terms of nominal values. Basically, the inflation itself is what makes calculation difficult. Those who wish to facilitate their calculating job by clinging to nominal values merely facilitate a job of miscalculating. Only those who calculate in real terms calculate correctly. And finally, if stabilization is being achieved, debtors should be glad that with the escalator provision they have settled for a variable inflation component.

11. The reminder that escalator clauses do not remove the causes of inflation and therefore cure only symptoms is in itself conclusive, but is not relevant in the framework of an anti-inflationary monetary policy. If the objection goes further and refers to real rather than monetary causes of inflation (for instance, to a shortage of supply caused by a crop failure or to an energy crisis), then we must remember that the temporary shortage means a slowing down of growth in real terms, of productivity gains and, therefore, of the increase in real incomes. One should expect monetary policy to take the slowdown into account by expanding the money supply less than would otherwise be appropriate. Thus, when food prices go up as a result of a crop failure, this should be offset by the absence of price increases that would otherwise be possible and by bringing about more price decreases. A monetary policy that does not take account of a shortage in supply becomes a contributing cause of inflation. So, even here, everything depends on monetary policy. If there are no escalator provisions and if monetary policy remains lax, there will probably be an inflationary wave; it will ebb after some time, when the nominal income claims will have lost enough of their real value. If many contracts with escalator clauses are in force, a lax monetary policy may indeed result in steeper price increases. All the heavier is the responsibility of monetary policy. This policy must make it clear that in any case, under monetary stability as well as under inflation, a

temporary supply shortage entails smaller increases in real wages, lower real profits, and lower real interest rates.[7]

12. A few critics think that escalator clauses tend to freeze the structure of prices and incomes. If I see things in their true light, this objection has three aspects.

First, the objection seems to say that escalator clauses make the conclusion of longer-term contracts attractive. The counterargument is simple: This, precisely, is the purpose. In the absence of escalator provisions, the uncertainty that accompanies an inflation produces short-term agreements, quite contrary to the basic interests of the market participants who, after all, do need security for longer-range planning and thus do need contracts that will remain binding over longer periods. In capital transactions, contract terms are shortened because interest rates depend on the rate of inflation and are therefore unpredictable for longer periods. As for collective wage agreements, in phases when the inflationary process is slowed down, employers fear that long-term contracts will be to their disadvantage; in phases of accelerating inflation, trade unions have analogous misgivings. In the first case, what is to be feared is an inordinately heavy cost burden. In the second, there is reason to fear the outbreak of wildcat strikes following upon an unanticipated decline in consumer purchasing power. It may well be true that negotiations about contracts with escalator clauses—like those about longer-term contracts in general—will be longer and harder because more is at stake, and also because, in this case, there is no chance that divergent expectations regarding the inflation will make it easier to reach an agreement. As a compensation, there will be no disappointments and none of the wildcat strikes that arise out of frustrated hopes. All in all, we can say that escalator provisions make the conclusion of an agreement as difficult, and its term of duration as long, as would be the case if the value of money were stable.

Second, the argument seems to say that escalator provisions in collective wage agreements impart too much rigidity into relationships among wages in the various sectors and industries. Here, too, the

---

[7] If the wage agreements contain escalator clauses, the loss in real income shows, during the terms of the agreements, in those incomes that are not fixed contractually, that is, in profits. Since, for them, escalator provisions are excluded by definition, the system is not blocked, as is sometimes believed. In the new wage bargaining it will come to light whether the entrepreneurs are able partially to offset the losses of profits by making smaller concessions on real wages. This would amount to an ex post acknowledgment of the fact that, due to the crop failure, the progress in productivity was smaller than had been assumed in the earlier agreements.

10

answer is that escalator clauses merely establish conditions exactly equivalent to what would obtain if the value of money were stable, and that, consequently, they cannot in the long run produce anything that would not exist under monetary stability as well. The essence of the objection presumably lies in the question of whether we need some minimum of inflation in order to bring about changes in the structure of real wages without nominal wages having to shrink anywhere. Primarily, the problem concerns the structurally weak sectors which, unless they are given watertight shelter from foreign competition, must lay off some workers anyway. In such sectors it may in general be impossible to secure the adoption of escalator provisions, even if they are permitted; at least it will be impossible to obtain them together with real wage increases fully reflecting the progress of productivity in the economy as a whole. If, in such cases, labor nevertheless presses for such real wage increases, layoffs will inevitably be accelerated, and the labor supply available to sectors having a positive growth potential will thereby be increased.

Moreover, escalator provisions may vary from case to case. In certain borderline situations it may be that the purchasing power of only part of the wage increases is guaranteed, or that compensation for a loss in purchasing power will be granted only with considerable delay. This would correspond to a situation where the workers, even in the face of an unexpectedly sharp decline in the value of money, do not feel strong enough to resort to wildcat strikes.

Third, behind the rigidity argument there could be the question of whether escalator provisions in collective wage agreements—if they stipulate full compensation for any loss in purchasing power and thus fix the real wage for the entire duration of the contract—might not cause undesired declines in employment. This point is to be taken very seriously. The objection implies that we need inflation because it corrects downward, in the degree required to avoid employment losses, those increases in real wages which the trade unions think they have secured by their demands for nominal wages. Basically, the argument says that it is necessary for us to have, permanently, an inflation that exceeds labor's expectations for inflation. Where this is the actual situation, a return to monetary stability seems anyway out of the question because of the huge losses in employment that would then be unavoidable. However, at least two points are open to doubt.

For one thing, labor is today so experienced in matters of inflation that an employment policy based on the Keynesian prescription, presupposing "money illusion," no longer holds out any promise of lasting success. For another, we must not overlook the fact that, in their wage bargaining, employees and trade unions do take the risk of unemployment into account—even if they do not admit it because they are interested, for reasons of negotiating tactics and political strategy, in placing the responsibility for full employment squarely upon the government. The notion that the volume of employment in an enterprise, in an industry, or in a region depends on the relation of real wages to labor productivity may be unpalatable, but if it is correct, as it undoubtedly is, it will spread, at least "under the counter." Here, escalator clauses may be helpful. By making negotiations about real wages possible, they offer to the parties in collective agreements the chance of eliminating unemployment risks, especially during a process of stabilization. On the other hand, whenever one oversteps the right boundary in real wages, the unemployment risk will become apparent, and the link just mentioned will stand out clearly. Nothing could contribute more to achieving, simultaneously, monetary stability and high-level employment than such an object lesson during the period of stabilization.[8]

13. Some political weight attaches to the objection that the decision to permit escalator provisions in a trotting inflation will be interpreted as an act of despair and as an indication of willingness to capitulate. This objection becomes irrelevant, however, when escalator clauses are permitted and introduced in order to make sure that a monetary policy program aiming at price stability will not be endangered by a worsening of the employment situation or by crises originating in overindebtedness.

14. A special problem is posed by declines in employment caused by a cost-oriented pricing policy on the part of business. Again and again we see business firms raising supply prices after wage negotiations and pointing out that they can absorb only part of the wage increases agreed upon—the part that is in line with the progress in productivity. The firms emphasize that the increased costs must be reflected in higher prices in order to keep profit margins intact. At the beginning of a "wage round," not only must all firms in one particular business sector expect wage increases of a specified extent, but often many other sectors have to face the same wage

---

[8] This reasoning is not invalidated by the consideration that in the central regions of Western Europe a steeper rise of real wages appears definitely desirable over the long pull if one wishes to curb the demand for foreign labor and to expedite the shift of job-creating investments from the central to the peripheral regions. See Giersch, "Beschäftigungspolitik ohne Geldillusion" [Employment policy without money illusion] in *Die Weltwirtschaft* (Tübingen), vol. 2 (1972), p. 127ff.

increases. Hence, one can foresee quickly by what percentage the cost level in the economy as a whole will rise and by what percentage, on the average, business will therefore raise supply prices. Assuming that the government will ensure the maintenance of full employment, they can also figure out quickly how much the incomes of the broad masses will rise, and how much room for increases in market prices will thereby be created on the demand side.

All they have to do is deduct the percentage increase in quantities supplied—which reflects the increase in productivity if the physical volume of work performed is assumed as constant—from the average percentage increase in wages, and take due account of a possible change in the rate of saving. If the rate of saving remains constant, there is as much room for price increases as the cost increases indicate. This means that, as a rule, the divisions in a business firm that calculate the costs of production and the divisions that analyze market conditions can take for their points of departure the same date relating to the economy as a whole. If the policy of the central bank brakes the expansion of the money supply, thereby narrowing the scope for passing on price increases while the pricing policy of business enterprises is dominated by the divisions calculating the costs of production, there will be shrinkages in quantities produced and supplied.

In these circumstances, escalator clauses in wage agreements have a major advantage which, to my knowledge, has not yet been mentioned in the literature. They weaken the influence upon business pricing policy of the divisions concerned with calculating costs, as compared with the influence of the divisions concerned with market analysis, and they force these latter divisions to use criteria other than wage increases. The arguments of the divisions calculating supply prices lose in weight because, under a regime of escalator clauses, the cost increase cannot be determined in advance but only ex post. This is an observation which entrepreneurs stress as an objection to escalator clauses, and which economists should stress as an important argument in favor of these clauses in a stabilization program. It is true that uncertainties of the kind mentioned also affect the divisions engaged in market analysis. But these divisions have another indicator for estimating how much price increase demand will absorb: the rate of increase in the supply of money minus the rate of increase in the real national product. If the divisions engaged in market analysis rather than the divisions engaged in calculating the costs of production gained the decisive influence on the actual pricing and if the market analysts concentrated on the increase in the volume of money rather than on the increase in wages, the goal of stabilization without appreciable negative responses of quantities might prove to be attainable.

15. In the Federal Republic, the discussion of escalator clauses turns on whether or not paragraph 3 of the Currency Act of 20 June 1948 should be applied. The main purpose of this provision, under which, in principle, permission is required for the use of escalator clauses, was to make the newly introduced D-Mark the only legal contract currency. If I see things correctly, it was—quite wrongly—considered necessary to expedite the movement away from barter transactions which had become quite popular before the currency reform and to prevent the use of foreign currencies. As a matter of principle, the Bundesbank has refused to permit the use of escalator clauses in the capital and money markets, and it has adopted a restrictive attitude with respect to such clauses in other fields also. Exceptions are long-term rent contracts (over at least ten years) and the sale of real estate to be paid for by an annuity over at least ten years or by a life annuity. This leads to the grotesque situation that anybody wishing to protect his money from the risk of inflation must first acquire real estate. Whether permission would be required for escalator provisions in wage contracts is a matter of controversy.

From a legal and political point of view, the prohibition of escalator clauses represents a restriction of the freedom of contract; it is an element of authoritarianism. So long as the rates of inflation were tolerable, the Bundesbank's tutelage over the citizens caused little resentment. But at present the situation is different. When contracting parties are uncertain about the future development of monetary values, when they are in the dark as to what they are fixing in real terms by fixing future payments in nominal terms, why should they not be given the option to eliminate the risk of inflation from their contractual relationship? All we have said so far points to the conclusion that such freedom could harm third parties only if monetary policy is not oriented toward stability. The agencies in charge should therefore regard the establishment of freedom of contract in matters involving money as a challenge to themselves. Our reference here is to the Bundesbank which, by issuing a general permission, could immediately and without difficulty make paragraph 3 of the Currency Act inoperative for all practical purposes.

16. Inflation-caused distortions appear also in public fees and fines that are expressed in absolute figures, and especially in progressive income taxes and in the exemptions and exclusions allowed by the tax law. It is only fair that exemptions and exclusions in systems of direct taxes should not lose their importance, thereby giving rise to

14

an unintended tax progression effect at the wrong place. Likewise, it is only fair that the rates of wage and income taxes be automatically lowered in order to ensure that tax progressivity will not begin at ever-decreasing real incomes, thus allowing the government to profit from the inflation through the progressivity of the tax structure. Furthermore, to the extent that interest receipts merely compensate for the loss in the value of property held in money form, they should be exempt from income tax. Otherwise, there would be an unintended taxation of property. Maybe this exemption would also give an impetus to saving and capital formation. On the other hand, interest payments on borrowed capital need to be deductible as costs only to the extent that they exceed the depreciation of the debts. As for tax-allowable depreciation charges on fixed assets, if the original asset values on which the depreciation charges are based were allowed to rise along with the rise of a general price index, we should be coming closer to depreciation allowances based on replacement costs—which is the economically correct method of computing these allowances. This step, too, would help to avoid an unintended taxation of property; moreover, it would probably induce many small- and medium-size firms to switch from the incorrect calculation based on nominal values to calculation in real terms. This would prevent them from making erroneous decisions that are conditioned by, and in turn aggravate, an ongoing inflation.

A program of stabilization without stagnation and loss of employment can be combined with tax reduction quite well. Alleviations in the field of taxation relieve the pressure of costs. This is especially true of wage taxes. In an ever-growing number of countries, the increases in these taxes that will take place under a progressive tax structure are being allowed for at the time when wage demands are being advanced. Often labor unions think not only in real terms but also in terms of disposable income. The loss of tax revenue resulting from an adjustment of the tax system must be offset by raising loans, preferably by issuing purchasing-power bonds, on the capital market. If it were to be expected that the substitution of proceeds from loans for revenues from taxes would have short-run inflationary effects, it would be necessary to resort to open-market policy by issuing additional loans and inactivating the resulting budgetary surpluses within the confines of the central banking system.

17. My final result can be summarized as follows. Contrary to widespread prejudices—which I myself could get rid of only after prolonged thinking, and which again and again prevail "intuitively" when for some time one does not think hard about the problem but

allows oneself to be impressed by conventional wisdom—I have reached the conclusion that in the present phase of the inflationary process escalator provisions would no longer have any accelerating effect on inflation. On the contrary, by forcing people to behave as they would if the value of money were again stable, they could help to avoid a stabilization crisis and thereby contribute to the actual restoration of monetary stability. In any case, however, a necessary precondition for a return to stability is a restrictive monetary policy.

Appendix: Scope and Forms of Escalator Clauses in Various Countries

1. Wages and Salaries

Denmark. Escalator clauses have been used since 1928. Since 1964 they have been in effect for nearly all blue-collar workers, white-collar workers, and employees in civil service.

The adjustment mechanism is based on the principle of a "sliding wage scale." Automatic wage adjustments (differentiated by wage brackets and sex) generally occur twice each year, whenever the consumer price index has risen at least three points since the last adjustment. Direct and indirect taxes, until 1963 contained in the consumer price index, are left out of account in the wage adjustments. Because of "wage drift" the adjustment for inflation for employees in private business is about one-third lower than the adjustment for persons employed in public service.

Italy. Escalator clauses have been in use since 1951 for all workers covered by collective bargaining agreements.

The adjustment mechanism is based on the "sliding wage scale" principle. Automatic wage adjustment (differentiated by wage brackets) occurs quarterly (agriculture, nonagricultural industry) and annually (public services). Quarterly adjustment is made whenever the cost-of-living index (as computed by a joint commission) has risen at least one point above the three-month average that occasioned the last adjustment.

Belgium. Escalator clauses have been used in mining since 1920. They have been introduced by collective agreements in all fields since 1948, and at present cover about 95 percent of all employees.

The adjustment mechanism is based on the general principle of the "sliding wage scale," but with differences among the different sectors.

The appendix was compiled by A. Ahnefeld and K.-H. Frank.

Automatic wage increases, as provided in collective agreements, occur whenever the rise in the consumer price index during two to four months has exceeded certain threshold values (2 to 2.5 percent) determined by a joint commission.

Finland. The coverage of escalator clauses was gradually extended to all employees, as well as to government-guaranteed incomes of farmers, between 1949 and 1968.

The adjustment mechanism is based on the principle of the "sliding wage scale." Until 1956 automatic proportional purchasing-power adjustment occurred whenever the consumer price index had risen at least five points within one quarter. During the period 1956-58, the following procedure was developed: If between June 1 and September 30 of any year the index rises at least five points, then the trade unions have the right to demand a purchasing-power adjustment. (If no agreement can be reached, the collective wage contract in effect may be terminated by notice before the stated date of expiration.)

Switzerland. Escalator clauses have been in use since the beginning of the 1960s. Today nearly all employees are covered.

In general the adjustment mechanism is based on the principle of "ex-ante indexing." As provided for in the collective agreement, new wage negotiations take place whenever consumer prices rise 2.5 to 3.5 percent. (This is the rule prevailing in private business.) But the "sliding wage scale" principle also is in use: After the consumer price index rises by a number of points fixed by agreement, an amount determined beforehand (and differentiated by wage classes) is paid as an addition to the wage. (This adjustment is made annually and is mostly for persons in the federal civil service.)

Netherlands. Escalator clauses have been permitted since 1965. At first they were restricted to collective agreements concluded for three years, but since the beginning of 1970 they have also been permitted in agreements with a one-year term.

The adjustment mechanism is based on the principle of "ex-ante indexing." Collective wage contracts contain an agreement about what rise in real wages should be effected within one year. If prices rise more than had been assumed, then either (a) resumption of collective wage bargaining ("flexible indexing") occurs, or (b) purchasing-power adjustment in the sense of the "sliding wage scale" principle ("limited indexing") is made.

Norway. Since the early 1950s, escalator provisions have been incorporated in collective wage agreements. Since 1968, such provisions have been part and parcel of the national wage agreements concluded for two years.

On the basis of a 1972 wage agreement, the rule is as follows: An addition to the wage payment is made whenever the consumer price index, in the course of some year, rises 5 percent above its level of two years earlier. In 1973, because of the steep price increase that year, the automatic wage adjustment was reduced from 70 percent to 45 percent of the rise in the consumer price index.

Iceland. Since June 1954 all employees have been covered by escalator clauses.

The adjustment mechanism is based on the principle of the "sliding wage scale." Automatic wage adjustment occurs every quarter, in proportion to the rise in prices.

France. Between 1952 and 1958 escalator clauses were in effect for statutory minimum wages. In 1958 there was a general prohibition of escalator clauses. Since 1968, escalator provisions have appeared in an ever-increasing number of collective agreements. Since 1969, civil service and public enterprises have been covered, as provided by "Accord Berliet."

The adjustment mechanism is based on the principle of "ex-ante indexing." When a collective agreement is concluded, a specified rate of inflation is assumed. If price increases are steeper than was assumed, an automatic wage increase occurs as under the "sliding wage scale" principle. In intervals of two months, automatic adjustments on the basis of the cost-of-living index are to be made whenever prices rise more than 5 percent.

Austria. Escalator clauses for wages in the public service sector have existed since 1967.

The adjustment mechanism is based on the principle of the "sliding wage scale." Wages are adjusted at the beginning of each year, in proportion to the rise in the cost of living, whenever the index rises 2.5 percent or more.

Great Britain. Escalator clauses have been in use since the beginning of the 1950s.

There were considerable differences among sectors, depending on provisions in collective agreements, in the adjustment mechanism. Both the "sliding wage scale" principle (with monthly, quarterly, or semiannual adjustments) and "ex-ante indexing" (in collective agreements with several years' terms, particularly in the metal industry) were used. At the end of 1973, the government encouraged threshold agreements in all industries within the framework of its incomes policy.

United States. Since 1948 there has been widespread use of escalator clauses in collective wage agreements with three-year terms. Since 1971 there has been even more widespread use, after some decline in the early 1960s. At present about 60 percent of all employees in manufacturing industries are covered.[9] Escalator clauses are particularly widespread in the automobile industry.

The adjustment mechanism is based on the principle of the "sliding wage scale." Adjustment is made monthly or quarterly, depending on the agreement. Wage rates are adjusted to the most recent level of the official consumer price index. In a number of cases, wages are tied not only to the consumer price index, but also to the development of productivity.

Brazil. Since 1964, escalator provisions have been in effect for minimum wages.

Wages are revised annually, based on the rise in the cost of living, but with differentiation by regions.

2. Money and Capital Transactions

France. During the period 1952-58, four government loans and one loan of the National Coal Authority contained escalator clauses. In October 1973 a government loan for the conversion of the Pinay loans of 1952-58 contained an escalator clause.

The amount to be paid as capital recovery on the Pinay loans is adjusted on the basis of the stock exchange quotation of the price of the twenty-franc gold coin (Napoléon). Ramadier loans are adjusted on the basis of the index of stock and bond prices in Paris. Capital values and interest payments on the loan of the National Coal Authority are adjusted on the basis of the wholesale price for coal.

Finland. Between 1946 and 1968 escalator clauses were included in credit transactions. Since 1953 and 1955 they have applied to loans and to savings deposits, respectively.

Adjustment of credits differs for different financial agencies. For insurance companies, national rent institutes, and the Postal Savings and Clearing Office, nominal values are adjusted by 25 to 50 percent of the increase in consumer or wholesale prices. For commercial banks,

---

[9] Translator's note: In 1972, in manufacturing industries about 17 percent of all employees and about 65 percent of all workers under collective agreements for 1,000 or more workers were covered by escalator clauses.

adjustment is usually indirect by escalating interest on debts. For credits underwritten by the government, nominal values are adjusted by 25 percent or 50 percent of the price increase; in the case of credits to large-scale export firms, adjustment is based on the exchange rate of the pound sterling.

For loans, compensation is 50 or 100 percent of value loss on interest and capital. The adjustment is based on the consumer price index, the wholesale price index, the export price index, or the official exchange rate between the Finnmark and the pound sterling (for government loans). The threshold value for compensation is between 1 percent and 5 percent of the price increase. There is a tax exemption for revenue from capital (for government loans).

Savings deposits of at least 300 Finnmarks deposited for one year are raised in nominal value in line with the rise in the consumer price index (if the index has risen at least 2 percent). There are various types of indexed accounts, characterized by one or several of the following provisions: an increase in nominal value by 50 or 100 percent of the price increase; interest rate reductions of ½ to 1½ percentage points as compared with nonindexed deposits; alleviation of tax load. (If 100 percent of the deposited value is protected, income tax and property tax are due, but if only 50 percent is protected, there is tax exemption; this was the rule until 1964.)

Denmark. Savings contracts securing old-age incomes are indexed.

The nominal value of the credit balance is raised in line with the increase in the consumer price index. The government refunds the difference betwen the amount saved and the value which, at payment time, results from the indexing.

Israel. Since 1955, bonds, bank deposits and credits have increasingly been subject to escalator clauses.

Usually capital repayment is increased in line with price increases, but the interest rate on the indexed loan, deposit or credit is below the interest rate on nonindexed loans, deposits or credits.

Brazil. Savings deposits, Treasury bills, public loans, and bank credits are all indexed.

For savings deposits, annual interest (6 percent) is earned on a capital value that is adjusted every quarter. For Treasury bills there is a monthly adjustment for the change in the value of money. For public loans, the nominal value of a loan is increased annually, in proportion to decline in value of money. For bank credits, interest payments are adjusted to changes in the rate of inflation.

3. Rents and Leases

Austria. Nearly all rent and lease contracts are indexed. Indicators used for the adjustment are the cost-of-living index, the index of building costs, and the index of wages as fixed by collective agreements.

Switzerland. Rent contracts concluded for five years or longer are indexed. Indicators used for the adjustment are the national consumer price index and the development of mortgage rates.

German Federal Republic. The Bundesbank permits the use of escalator clauses in rent contracts if the term of the contract is at least ten years, and if adjustment is provided for price declines as well as for price increases. In general the consumer price index is the indicator used for the adjustment.

Brazil. All rent and lease contracts are indexed. An increase in consumer prices or an increase in statutory minimum wages are the bases of the adjustment.

4. Social Insurance

Belgium. All social insurance benefits and premiums are raised in proportion to the rise of consumer prices (if the rise is at least 2.5 percent), but with a two-month lag.

Denmark, Sweden, Norway, Finland. Basic and supplementary benefits are indexed. In most instances, the annual increase in insurance benefits is in proportion to the rise of consumer prices.

Switzerland. Social insurance benefits paid by the Swiss Accident Insurance Board and by the military and civilian Work Service Establishment contain escalator clauses. Increases are automatic whenever the price index rises at least 5 percent.

Austria. There have been escalator provisions for social insurance and welfare benefits since 1965. Benefits are raised in line with the rise in wages.

United States. Benefits paid by some pension insurance plans are indexed on the basis of either the index of consumer prices or the index of hourly earnings. Pensions for civil service employees and military personnel are raised whenever consumer prices have risen at least 3 percent in three consecutive months.

Brazil. Social insurance benefits are raised in proportion to increases in statutory minimum wages.

5. Life Insurance Policies

France, Great Britain, Sweden, Finland, Italy, Austria, Netherlands, Israel, United States. Escalator clauses in life insurance plans are in wide use in only a few of these countries. There are two important ways in which life insurance policies are indexed. In the case of policies with true escalator clauses, both benefits and premiums are indexed. (This calls for indexing of the property values in which the insurance companies invest their premium reserves.) In the case of policies with adjustment provisions that do not represent true escalator clauses, supplementary insurance contracts are concluded occasionally in order to compensate for the decline in the purchasing power of money that has taken place.

6. Taxation

Denmark. Current rules for indexing income taxes have been in effect since the end of 1972. In accordance with a ruling anchored in law, personal exemptions and the incomes recorded in tax rate schedules as falling in brackets taxable at specified rates are automatically adjusted upward each year. The basis for the adjustment is the level of the cost-of-living index in January of the year preceding the tax year. The adjustment is not "sliding" but step-wise, taking place when the price increase relative to the base year has reached 3 percent, 6 percent, 9 percent, and so on.

Netherlands. Income taxes are indexed. Each year, the incomes recorded in tax rate schedules as falling in brackets taxable at specified rates are to be adjusted upward by a so-called tax table correction multiplier reflecting the rise in the cost of living in the preceding year. The cost-of-living index is to be adjusted by eliminating the price-increasing effect of indirect taxes and the price-lowering effect of subsidies. The minister of finance may decree that the adjustment to the price level be less than 100 percent.

France. Income taxes have been indexed since 1968. By resolution of the National Assembly, the income tax schedule changes whenever the price level has risen more than 5 percent per year.

Switzerland. Periodic adjustment of the tax burden is anchored in a general provision of the Federal Constitution. Income taxes, revenue taxes, and property taxes are indexed. There are different rules in the tax laws of different cantons: Whenever the cost-of-living index exceeds—by some specified percentage (5 or 10 percent)—the level it had in some base year, an adjustment is made. It is either a downward adjustment, in proportion to the general price increase, of the taxpayer's gross income as underlying the derivation of his tax liability (the "deflation" method) or an upward adjustment, by the rate of the general price increase, of all allowable (maximum) deductions, all exemptions and exclusions, and the incomes recorded in tax rate schedules as falling in brackets taxable at specified rates (the "blowup" method).

Brazil. Income taxes and profits taxes are indexed. Tax-allowable exemptions and deductions and incomes recorded in tax rate schedules as taxable at specified rates are raised by a multiplier determined by the National Economic Council. When profit is to be determined on the basis of a balance sheet, the values of fixed and non-fixed assets are raised in proportions determined by the year of acquisition and the price increase since that year.

2
MONETARY CORRECTION
Milton Friedman

Synopsis

There is no technical problem about how to end inflation (Section 1). The real obstacles are political, not technical.

Ending inflation would deprive government of revenue it now obtains without legislation (Section 2). Replacing this revenue will require government to reduce expenditures, raise explicit taxes, or borrow additional sums from the public—all politically unattractive. I do not know any way to avoid this obstacle.

Ending inflation would also have the side effect of producing a temporary, though perhaps fairly protracted, period of economic recession or slowdown and of relatively high unemployment. The political will is today lacking to accept that side effect. Experience suggests that its occurrence would instead produce an overreaction involving accelerated government spending and monetary growth that in its turn would produce the initial side effect of an unsustainable boom followed by accelerated inflation. These side effects of changes in the rate of inflation arise because of the time it takes for the community to adjust itself to changed rates of growth of spending. The time delay distorts relative prices, the structure of production, and the level of employment. In turn, it takes time to correct these distortions (Section 3).

The side effects of changes in the rate of inflation can be substantially reduced by encouraging the widespread use of price escalator clauses in private and governmental contracts. Such arrangements

This essay originally appeared in a briefer version in *Fortune* Magazine, July 1974 (© Time Inc., 1974), and, in its present form, as Occasional Paper No. 41 of the Institute of Economic Affairs, London (© Institute of Economic Affairs, 1974). Permission to reprint is gratefully acknowledged.

involve deliberately eschewing some of the advantages of the use of money and hence are not good in and of themselves. They are simply a lesser evil than a badly managed money. The widespread use of escalator clauses would not by itself either increase or decrease the rate of inflation. But it would reduce the revenue that government acquires from inflation—which also means that government would have less incentive to inflate. More important, it would reduce the initial adverse side effects on output and employment of effective measures to end inflation (Section 4).

The use of escalator clauses in government contracts—taxation, borrowing, hiring, purchasing—should be required by law. Their use in private contracts should be permitted and enforceable at law but should be voluntary. The two are related because government adoption of escalator clauses, particularly in taxes, would remove serious impediments to their private adoption (Section 5).

Objections to widespread escalation mostly reflect misconceptions about its effects. These misconceptions reflect the same confusion between relative prices and absolute prices that is responsible for many of the adverse effects of accelerated inflation or deflation and for misconceptions about the cause and cure of inflation (Section 6).

1. The Technical Cause and Cure of Inflation

Short-run changes in both particular prices and in the general level of prices may have many sources. But long-continued inflation is always and everywhere a monetary phenomenon that arises from a more rapid expansion in the quantity of money than in total output[1] —though I hasten to add that the exact rate of inflation is not precisely or mechanically linked to the exact rate of monetary growth. (The accompanying figure plots consumer prices in the United States and the ratio of the quantity of money to output over the period 1962-73.)

This statement is only a first step towards an understanding of the causes of any particular inflation. It must be completed by an explanation of the reason for the rapid monetary growth. The rapid monetary growth that produced inflation in the United States from 1848 to 1860 reflected gold discoveries in California. The rapid monetary growth that produced world inflation from 1890 to 1914 reflected

---

[1] This is a bit of an oversimplification, because a fully defensible statement would have to allow for autonomous changes in velocity, that is, in the demand for real balances, and would have to specify the precise definition of "money." But I know of no case in which these qualifications are of critical importance.

Figure 1

MONEY AND PRICES, 1962-1973

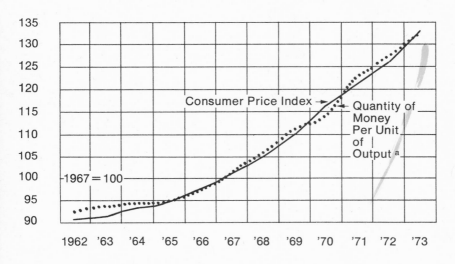

a There is a delay in the impact of a change in the quantity of money. Therefore, the money index measures the quantity of money (M_2) for the fiscal year ending 30 June while output (real GNP) is for the calendar year.
Source: *Newsweek*, 24 June 1974. © Newsweek Inc., 1974.

the perfection of the cyanide process for extracting gold from low-grade ore. The rapid monetary growth that has time and again produced wartime inflation has reflected the use of the printing press or its equivalent to finance wartime government spending.

Causes of worldwide growth of money supply. Under modern conditions, the quantity of money is determined by governmental monetary authorities. The accelerated increase in the quantity of money throughout the world in the past decade, which is responsible for the recent acceleration of inflation, has reflected a number of causes:

—the attempt to maintain fixed exchange rates, which induced some countries, notably Germany and Japan, to "import" inflation from the United States;

—the expansion in the role of government, and the reluctance to impose explicit taxes, which has induced many governments to use the implicit tax of inflation; and

—the commitment of governments to a policy of full employment, which has led them to overreact to temporary recessions by measures leading to rapid monetary growth.

Long-continued inflation can be ended only by a reduction in the rate of monetary growth. But, again, this statement is only a first step. The measures that can be used to reduce the rate of monetary growth may vary widely depending on the sources of the excess growth and the institutions of the country in question. For example, if monetary growth has reflected the financing of government expenditures by the printing press, it can be ended by reducing government spending, raising taxes, or financing the deficit in the government budget by borrowing from the public rather than by creating money. But the third of these methods may not be available for a country that does not have well-developed security markets. And all hyper-inflations have reflected governments so impotent and disorganized as to be unable to employ the method of raising taxes.

Importance—and limitations—of fiscal policy. As these comments imply, fiscal policy may play an important role in producing and curing inflation. Its influence is primarily through its effect on the quantity of money. But its influence can be offset by other forces affecting the quantity of money. Large government surpluses in the United States in 1919 and 1920 did not prevent rapid inflation because they were accompanied by rapid monetary growth which financed private spending. Large government deficits in the United States in 1931 to 1933 did not produce rapid inflation or prevent severe deflation because they were accompanied by a sharp decline in the quantity of money which sharply reduced private spending.

What matters for inflation is not simply the rate of monetary growth but the rate of growth relative to the rate of growth of output, and, in a more sophisticated presentation, relative to the rate of growth in the demand for real money balances at a constant level (or rate of change) of prices. This relationship has led many commentators to emphasize the role of "productivity," arguing that inflation reflects a decline in productivity (or its rate of growth) and that a cure requires an increase in productivity (or its rate of growth). Though the role of output growth is, in principle, strictly symmetrical to the role of monetary growth, the quantitative orders of magnitude are wholly different. For any given country, over any period longer than a few years, the rate of output growth is unlikely to vary by more than a few percentage points—it would take a major structural change, for example, to raise the rate of growth of output in the United States by two percentage points, from, say, 3–4 percent per year to 5–6 percent. On the other hand, the rate of monetary growth can and does vary over a much wider range—it can easily go from 3 or 4 percent per year to 20 percent per year. As a matter of experience, therefore, long-continued inflation is dominated by monetary changes rather than by changes in output.

The importance of the simple proposition in this section is that no measures are likely to produce long-continued inflation or to cure long-continued inflation unless they affect the long-term rate of monetary growth.

2. Government Revenue from Inflation

Since time immemorial, the major source of inflation has been the sovereign's attempt to acquire resources to wage war, to construct monuments, or for other purposes. Inflation has been irresistibly attractive to sovereigns because it is a hidden tax that at first appears painless or even pleasant, and, above all, because it is a tax that can be imposed without specific legislation. It is truly taxation without representation.

The revenue yield from inflation takes three major forms:

(1) Additional government-created fiat money. Since ancient times, sovereigns have debased coinage by replacing silver or gold with base metals.[2] Later, paper currency supplemented token coins. More recently still, book entries at central banks (misleadingly called deposits) have been added. Governments use the fiat money that they issue to finance expenditures or repay debt. In addition, the fiat money serves as a base on which the banking system creates additional money in the form of bank deposits. In the calendar year 1973 the U.S. government realized $8 billion from this source—$6 billion more currency and coin in circulation on 31 December 1973 than on 31 December 1972, and over $2 billion in additional deposits at Federal Reserve Banks.[3]

---

[2] One historian of money describes the debasement of the Roman *denarius* from an initially full-bodied silver coin until, by the time of Emperor Diocletian (300 AD), it had become "practically a copper coin being only slightly washed with silver" (Rupert J. Ederer, *The Evolution of Money* [Washington, D. C.: Public Affairs Press, 1964], p. 88). We have gone farther than Diocletian. We wash our copper coins now with nickel, so that not even a trace of silver remains.

[3] Excluding Treasury deposits. Nominally, the Federal Reserve Banks are owned by their member banks. This is a pure formality. In practice the Federal Reserve System is part of the government. It earns "income" in the form of "interest" paid to it by the U.S. Treasury on government securities; it returns the excess of such "interest" over operating expenses to the Treasury. Economic understanding is promoted and confusion avoided by consolidating the accounts of the Federal Reserve System with those of the Treasury.

(2) Windfall tax yield. Inflation increases the yield of the personal and corporate income tax by pushing individuals and corporations into higher income groups, generating artificial (paper) capital gains on which taxes must be paid, and rendering permitted depreciation allowances inadequate to replace capital, so taxing a return *of* capital to shareholders as if it were a return *on* capital. For the corporation tax alone, the U.S. government realized in 1973 nearly $13 billion from this source.[4]

(3) Reduction in the real amount of outstanding national debt. Much of this debt was issued at yields that did not allow for current rates of inflation. On a conservative estimate, the U.S. government realized in 1973 something like $5 billion from this source.[5]

All told, the U.S. government's revenue from inflation totalled more than $25 billion in 1973. Ending inflation would end this source of revenue. Government would have to reduce expenditures, increase explicit taxes, or borrow additional funds from the public at whatever interest rate would clear the market. None of these courses is politically attractive.

3. Side Effects on Output and Employment

Acute appendicitis is accompanied by a high fever; the removal of the appendix will require that the patient stay in bed for some days. But the fever is not the cause of the appendicitis and bed rest is not the cure. Both are side effects.

The analogy with inflation is striking. The boom that typically accompanies the onset of accelerated inflation is not the cause of the inflation but a side effect; the recession and unemployment that typically accompany the reduction of inflation are not the cure but a side effect. There are many ways to increase unemployment that would exacerbate inflation rather than cure it.

---

[4] Inflation produced an overstatement of 1973 corporate profits by more than $26 billion through spurious profits on inventories and underdepreciation, according to Department of Commerce estimates summarized by George Terborgh, *Inflation and Profits* (Washington, D. C.: Machinery and Allied Products Institute, revised, 2 April 1974). At a 48 percent corporate tax rate, the additional tax paid was about $12.8 billion. In addition, corporate capital gains were undoubtedly overstated.

[5] Total interest paid on the roughly $260 billion of federal debt held by the public was at an average rate of about 5.7 percent. A 1973 market rate would have been about two percentage points higher, which means that the revenue to the government on this basis was about $5 billion. However, in retrospect, it seems clear that 1973 market rates did not adequately allow for inflation.

Time-lags lead to side effects. Higher inflation reflects an acceleration in the growth rate of total money spending. Ending inflation requires a deceleration in the growth rate of total spending. The reason for the side effects from such changes in total spending—both the boom which is generally regarded as a desirable side effect and the recession which is uniformly regarded as an undesirable side effect—is the time delay between an increased or decreased rate of growth of total money spending and the full adjustment of output and prices to that changed rate of growth of total spending.

Essentially the same side effects will arise whatever may be the cause of the changed growth rate in total spending—just as a high fever accompanies many different diseases and bed rest many different cures. When nonmonetary forces produce brief fluctuations in the rate of growth of total spending, the same side effects occur. Also, if there is some cause other than unduly rapid monetary growth for long-continued inflation, or some cure other than reduced monetary growth, that cause and that cure will operate largely by affecting the growth rate in total money spending, and hence will produce much the same side effects. Similarly, the measures proposed later to reduce the adverse side effects of ending inflation will be effective whatever the cause and whatever the cure.

Hence the rest of this essay is relevant, even if you do not accept my monetarist view as expressed in Section 1.

Expectations slow to change. When total spending slows down, each producer separately tends to regard the reduction in the demand for his product as special to him, and to hope that it is temporary. He is inclined to meet it primarily by reducing output or accumulating inventory, not by shading prices. Only after a time lag will he start to shade prices. Similarly, any of his workers who are laid off are likely to react by waiting to be recalled or by seeking jobs elsewhere, not by moderating wage demands or expectations. A slowdown in total spending will therefore tend to be reflected initially in a widespread slowdown in output and employment and an increase in inventories. It will take some time before these responses lead in turn to widespread reductions in the rate of inflation and the rate of increase in wages. It will take still more time before *expectations* about inflation are revised and the revised expectations encourage a resumption of employment and output.

This is a highly simplified picture. Different activities have different time-speeds of adjustment. Some prices, wages and production schedules are fixed a long time in advance; others can be adjusted promptly. As a result, a slowdown of total spending produces substantial shifts in *relative* prices, which will sooner or later have to be corrected; the correction in turn will cause economic disturbances.

For the United States, study of monetary history[6] indicates that the time delay between a change in the rate of monetary growth and a corresponding change in the rate of growth of total spending and total output has averaged six to nine months; between the change in the rate of growth of spending and of prices, twelve to eighteen months. Accordingly, the total delay between a change in monetary growth and in the rate of inflation has been about two years.[7] For the U.K., the available evidence indicates that the time delay is roughly the same as for the U.S.

Serious effects on lending. The time delay and resultant distortion are particularly clear for loans, where the distinction between *nominal* and *real* is especially important. Suppose you lend someone $100 in return for a promise to pay you $110 a year later. Neglect any possibility of default. What interest rate have you received? In dollars, 10 percent. But if prices have risen by 10 percent during the year, the $110 will buy only as much as the $100 would have done a year earlier. Your *real* return is nil. Indeed, if, as is true today, the $10 nominal return is subject to income tax, your *real* return is negative. You end up with *less* than you started with.

If you entered into a mortgage some years back, you may have paid 5 or 6 percent. Given the inflation of the past few years, your effective *real* rate may have been nil. The rising price level probably raised the value of your property by as much as, or more than, the interest you paid. The lender in turn received a *real* return of nil—or a negative return if he was liable to tax. Similarly, consider someone who today takes out a mortgage at 11 percent or more. Suppose economic policy were successful in bringing inflation down to nil. He would be in severe difficulties (unless of course the rate were reduced), and the lender would have received a wholly unexpected gain.

Failure of political will. Such side effects constitute, I believe, the most important political obstacle to ending inflation, given, first, the commitment on the part of the U.S., U.K., and most other govern-

---

[6] Milton Friedman, *The Optimum Quantity of Money* (London: Macmillan, 1969), Chapters 10, 11 and 12; and "Letter on Monetary Policy," *Review*, Federal Reserve Bank of Saint Louis, March 1974. Also, A. James Meigs, *Money Matters* (New York: Harper & Row, 1972), Chapter 6.

[7] This is precisely what W. Stanley Jevons estimated it to be: "An expansion of the currency occurs one or two years prior to a rise of prices." (*Investigations into Currency and Finance* [London: Macmillan, 1884], p. 107.)

ments to "full employment," second, the failure of the public at large to recognize the inevitable if temporary side effects of ending inflation, and third, the unwillingness or inability of political leaders to persuade the public to accept these side effects.

Some years ago, when inflation was much lower than now, I believed that the readjustment required was sufficiently mild and brief to be politically feasible. But unfortunately in the United States the opportunity was cast aside on 15 August 1971, when President Nixon reversed economic policy by imposing a price and wage freeze and encouraging expansive monetary and fiscal policy. At the time, we were well on the way to ending inflation without severe side effects. At the cost of the mild 1970 recession, the annual rate of inflation had been reduced from over 6 percent to 4.5 percent and was still declining. The economy was slowly recovering from that recession. Had the nation had the will—for President Nixon was reflecting a widespread national consensus when he reversed policy—another year of continued monetary restraint and of slow expansion would probably have turned the trick. As it was, the 1970 recession was a masochistic exercise rather than a side effect of a successful cure.

Inflation in the United States is currently (mid-1974) far worse than in August 1971. The 14 percent rate in the first quarter of 1974 was doubtless a temporary bubble, but, even on the most optimistic view, inflation is not likely to fall below 6 percent during the coming year. Starting from that level, and with inflationary expectations even more deeply entrenched, an effective policy to end inflation would entail as a side effect a considerably more severe and protracted recession than we experienced in 1970. The political will to accept such a recession, without reversing policy and restimulating inflation, is simply not present.

What then? If we—and probably Britain and other countries similarly placed—do nothing, we shall suffer even higher rates of inflation—not continuously, but in spurts as we overreact to temporary recessions. Sooner or later, the public will get fed up, will demand effective action, and we shall then have a really severe recession.

4. Easing the Side Effects

How can we make it politically feasible to end inflation much sooner? As I see it, inflation can be ended sooner only by adopting measures that will reduce the side effects from ending it. These side effects fundamentally reflect distortions introduced into *relative* prices by *unanticipated* inflation or deflation, distortions that arise because contracts are entered into in terms of *nominal* prices under mistaken perceptions about the likely course of inflation.

Escalator clauses: an illustration. The way to reduce these side effects is to make contracts in *real*, not nominal, terms. This can be done by the widespread use of escalator clauses.

Let me illustrate. In 1967 General Motors and the United Automobile Workers Union reached a wage agreement for a three-year period. At the time, prices had been relatively stable, consumer prices having risen at the average rate of 2.5 percent in the preceding three years. The wage agreement was presumably based on an expectation by both General Motors and the union that prices would continue to rise at 2.5 percent or less. That expectation was not realized. From 1967 to 1970, prices rose at an average annual rate of 5.2 percent. The result was that General Motors paid *real* wages that were increasingly lower than the levels both parties had expected. The unexpected fall in real wages was a stimulus to General Motors, and no doubt led it to produce at a higher rate than otherwise. Initially, the unexpected fall in real wages was no deterrent to workers, since it took some time before they recognized that the accelerated rise in consumer prices was more than a transitory phenomenon. But by 1970 they were certainly aware that their real wages were less than they had bargained for.

The result was a strike in late 1970, settled by a wage agreement that provided (1) a very large increase in the initial year, (2) much smaller increases for the next two years, and (3) a cost-of-living escalator clause. The contract was widely characterized as "inflationary." It was no such thing. The large initial year increase simply made up for the effect of the past unanticipated inflation. It restored *real wages* to the levels at which both parties had expected them to be. The escalator clause was designed to prevent a future similar distortion, and it has done so.

This General Motors example illustrates a side effect of unanticipated inflation. Suppose the same contract had been reached in 1967 but that the rate of inflation, instead of accelerating, had declined from 2.5 percent to nil. Real wages would then have risen above the level both parties had anticipated; General Motors would have been driven to reduce output and employment; the workers would have welcomed the unexpectedly high real wage rate but would have deplored the lower employment; when contract renewal was due, the union, not General Motors, would have been in a weak bargaining position.

An escalator clause which works both up and down would have prevented both the actual side effects from unanticipated inflation and the hypothetical side effects from unanticipated deflation. It would have enabled employers and employees to bargain in terms of the conditions of their own industry without having also to guess what was going to happen to prices in general, because both General Motors and the union would have been protected against either more rapid inflation or less rapid inflation.

Useful though they are, widespread escalator clauses are not a panacea. It is impossible to escalate *all* contracts (consider, for example, paper currency), and costly to escalate many. A powerful advantage of using money is precisely the ability to carry on transactions cheaply and efficiently, and universal escalator clauses reduce this advantage. Far better to have no inflation and no escalator clauses. But that alternative is not currently available.

Origins of the escalator: the "tabular standard." Let me note also that the widespread use of escalator clauses is not a new or untried idea. It dates back to at least 1707, when a Cambridge don, William Fleetwood, estimated the change in prices over a 600-year period in order to calculate comparable limits on outside income that college fellows were permitted to receive. It was suggested explicitly in 1807 by an English writer on money, John Wheatley. It was spelled out in considerable detail and recommended enthusiastically in 1886 by the great English economist, Alfred Marshall.[8] The great American economist Irving Fisher not only favored the "tabular standard"—as the proposal for widespread indexation was labelled nearly two centuries ago—but also persuaded a manufacturing company that he helped to found to issue a purchasing-power security as long ago as 1925. Interest in the "tabular standard" was the major factor accounting for the development of index numbers of prices. In recent years, the "tabular standard" has been adopted by Brazil on a wider scale than I would recommend for the United States. It has been adopted on a smaller scale by Canada, Israel, and many other countries.[9]

5. The Specific Proposal

For the United States, my specific proposal has two parts, one for the federal government, one for the rest of the economy. For the federal

---

[8] His discussion is reproduced in an appendix to this paper.

[9] A useful survey is in Robert P. Collier, *Purchasing Power Bonds and Other Escalated Contracts* (Taipei, Taiwan: Buffalo Book Co., 1969; distributed in the United States by the Utah State University Press, Logan, Utah).

government, I propose that escalator clauses be legislated; for the rest of the economy, that they be voluntary but that any legal obstacles be removed. The question of which index number to use in such escalator clauses is important but not critical. As Alfred Marshall said in 1886, "A perfectly exact measure of purchasing power is not only unattainable, but even unthinkable." For the United States, as a matter of convenience, I would use the cost-of-living index number calculated by the Bureau of Labor Statistics.

The Government. The U.S. government has already adopted escalation for social security payments, retirement benefits to federal employees, wages of many government employees, and perhaps some other items. Taxes which are expressed as fixed percentages of price or other value base are escalated automatically. The key additional requirement is for escalator clauses in the personal and corporate income tax and in government securities.

The personal tax.[10] Minor details aside, four revisions are called for:

(1) The personal exemption, the standard deduction, and the low-income allowance should be expressed not as a given number of dollars, but as a given number of dollars multiplied by the ratio of a price index for the year in question to the index for the base year in which "indexation" starts. For example, if in the first year prices rise by 10 percent, then the present amounts should be multiplied by 110/100 or 1.10.

(2) The brackets in the tax tables should be adjusted similarly, so that, in the examples given, 0–$500 would become 0–$550, and so on.
(These two measures have been adopted by Canada.)

(3) The base for calculating capital gains should be multiplied by the ratio of the price index in the year of sale to the price index in the year of purchase. This would prevent the taxing of non-existent, purely paper capital gains.

(4) The base for calculating depreciation on fixed capital assets should be adjusted in the same way as the base for calculating capital gains.

The corporate tax.[10] Similar revisions should be made in the corporate tax:

---

[10] These tax and borrowing measures are all contained in a bill introduced by Senator James Buckley in April 1974.

(1) The present $25,000 dividing line between normal tax and surtax should be replaced by that sum multiplied by a price index number.

(2) The cost of inventories used in sales should be adjusted to eliminate book profit (or losses) resulting from changes in prices between initial purchase and final sale.

(3) The base for calculating capital gains and depreciation of fixed capital assets should be adjusted as for the personal tax.

Government securities.[10] Except for short-term bills and notes, all government securities should be issued in purchasing-power form. (For example, Series E bonds should promise a redemption value equal to the product of the face value calculated at, say, 3 percent per year and the ratio of the price index in the year of redemption to the price index in the year of purchase.) Coupon securities should carry coupons redeemable for the face amount multiplied by the relevant price ratio, and bear a maturity value equal to the face amount similarly multiplied by the relevant price ratio.

These changes in taxes and in borrowing would reduce both the incentive for government to resort to inflation and the side effects of changes in the rate of inflation on the private economy. But they are called for also by elementary principles of ethics, justice, and representative government, which is why I propose making them permanent.

Taxation inflated to record levels. As a result largely of inflation produced by government in the United States, the U.K. and elsewhere, personal income taxes are today heavier than during the peak of Second World War financing, despite several "reductions" in tax rates. Personal exemptions in real terms are at a record low level. The taxes levied on persons in different economic circumstances deviate widely from the taxes explicitly intended to apply to them. Government has been in the enviable position of imposing higher taxes while appearing to reduce taxes. The less enviable result has been a wholly arbitrary distribution of the higher taxes.

As for government borrowing, the savings bond campaigns of the U.S. and U.K. treasuries have been the largest bucket-shop operations ever engaged in. This is not a recent development. In responding to a questionnaire of the Joint Economic Committee of Congress, I wrote as early as 1951:

> I strongly favor the issuance of a purchasing-power bond on two grounds: (a) It would provide a means for lower- and middle-income groups to protect their capital against the ravages of inflation. This group has almost no effective

means of doing so now. It seems to me equitable and socially desirable that they should. (b) It would permit the Treasury to sell bonds without engaging in advertising and promotion that at best is highly misleading, at worst, close to being downright immoral. The Treasury urges people to buy bonds as a means of securing their future. Is the implicit promise one that it can make in good faith, in light of past experience of purchasers of such bonds who have seen their purchasing power eaten away by price rises? If it can be, there is no cost involved in making the promise explicit by adding a purchasing-power guarantee. If it cannot be, it seems to me intolerable that an agency of the public deliberately mislead the public.

Surely the experience of the nearly quarter-century since these words were written reinforces their pertinence. Essentially every purchaser of savings bonds or, indeed, almost any other long-term Treasury security during that period, has paid for the privilege of lending to the government: the supposed "interest" he has received has not compensated for the decline in the purchasing power of the principal, and, to add insult to injury, he has had to pay tax on the paper interest. And the inflation which has sheared the innocent lambs has been produced by the government which benefits from the shearing.

It is a mystery to me—and a depressing commentary on either the understanding or the sense of social responsibility of businessmen (I say business*men*, not business)—that year after year eminent and honorable business leaders have been willing to aid and abet this bucket-shop operation by joining committees to promote the sale of U.S. saving bonds or by providing facilities for payroll deductions for their employees who buy them.

The Private Economy. Private use of escalator clauses is an expedient that has no permanent role, if government manages money responsibly. Hence I favor keeping private use voluntary in order to promote its self-destruction if that happy event arrives.

No legislation is required for the private adoption of escalator clauses, which are now widespread. Something over 5 million U.S. workers are covered by union contracts with automatic escalator clauses, and there must be many nonunion workers who have similar implicit or explicit agreements with their employers. Many contracts for future delivery of products contain provisions for adjustment of the final selling price either for specific changes in costs or for general price changes. Many rental contracts for business premises are expressed as a percentage of gross or net receipts, which means that they have an implicit escalator clause. This is equally true for percentage royalty payments and for automobile insurance policies that pay the cost of repairing damage. Some insurance companies issue fire insurance policies the face value of which is automatically adjusted for inflation. No doubt there are many more examples of which I am ignorant.

It is highly desirable that escalator clauses should be incorporated in a far wider range of wage agreements, contracts for future delivery of products, and financial transactions involving borrowing and lending. The first two are entirely straightforward extensions of existing practices. The third is more novel.

"Indexation" for corporate loans. The arrangements suggested for government borrowing would apply equally to long-term borrowing by private enterprises. Instead of issuing a security promising to pay, say, interest of 9 percent per year and to repay $1,000 at the end of five years, the XYZ company could promise to pay 3 percent plus the rate of inflation each year and to repay $1,000 at the end of five years. Alternatively, it could promise to pay each year 3 percent times the ratio of the price index in that year to the price index in the year the security was issued and to repay at the end of five years $1,000 times the corresponding price ratio for the fifth year. (The alternative methods are illustrated in Table 1.) If there is inflation, the first

---

Table 1

HYPOTHETICAL INDEXED BOND [a]

| Year | U.S. Consumer Price Level | | Method 1 | Method 2 |
	Index [b]	Percent change		
			Interest payments each year	
1968	100.0	—	—	—
1969	105.4	5.4	$84	$31.62
1970	111.6	5.9	89	33.48
1971	116.4	4.3	73	34.92
1972	120.2	3.3	63	36.06
1973	127.7	6.2	92	38.31
			Repayment of principal in 1973	
			$1,000	$1,277

a $1,000 five-year bond issued in 1968 at a real rate of 3 percent.

b U.S. consumer price index, 1968 = 100 (obtained from officially published index with 1967 = 100 by dividing by 1968 value of 104.2).

method implicitly involves amortizing part of the real value of the bond over the five-year period; the second involves currently paying interest only, at a constant real rate, and repaying the whole principal in *real* value at the end of the five years.

So far, there has been little incentive for private borrowers to issue such securities. The delay in adjusting anticipations about inflation to the actual acceleration of inflation has meant that interest rates on long-term bonds have been extremely low in real terms. Almost all enterprises that have issued bonds in the past decade have done extremely well—the rate of inflation has often exceeded the interest rate they had to pay, making the real cost negative.

Lenders' changing expectations. Three factors could change this situation: (1) As lenders, who have been the losers so far, come to have more accurate expectations of inflation, borrowers will have to pay rates high enough to compensate for the actual inflation. (2) Government purchasing-power securities might prove so attractive that competition would force private enterprises to do the same. (3) Related to (2), if it became clear that there was a real possibility that government would follow effective policies to stem inflation, borrowing would no longer be a one-way street. Enterprises would become concerned that they might become locked into high interest-rate loans. They might then have more interest in protecting themselves against inflation.

Businessmen's fears unwarranted. One question has invariably been raised when I have discussed this possibility with corporate executives: "Is it not too risky for us to undertake an open-ended commitment? At least with fixed nominal rates we know what our obligations are." This is a natural query from businessmen reared in an environment in which a roughly stable price level was taken for granted. But in a world of *varying* rates of inflation, the *fixed*-rate agreement is the more risky agreement. To quote Alfred Marshall again, "Once it [the tabular standard] has become familiar none but gamblers would lend or borrow on any other terms, at all events for long periods."

The money receipts of most businesses vary with inflation. If inflation is high, their receipts in money terms are high and they can pay the escalated rate of interest; if inflation is low, their receipts are low and they will find it easier to pay the low rate with the adjustment for inflation than a fixed but high rate; and similarly at the time of redemption.

The crucial point is the relation between assets and liabilities. Currently, for many enterprises, their assets, including goodwill, are real in the sense that their money value will rise or fall with the general price level, but their liabilities tend to be nominal, that is, fixed in money terms. Accordingly, these enterprises benefit from inflation at a higher rate than was anticipated when the nominal liabilities were acquired and are harmed by inflation at a lower rate than was anticipated. If assets and liabilities were to match, such enterprises would be protected against either event.

Home mortgages—threat of "major crisis." A related yet somewhat different case is provided by financial intermediaries. Consider savings and loan associations and mutual savings banks. Both their assets (primarily home mortgages) and their liabilities (due to shareholders or depositors) are expressed in money terms. But they differ in time duration. The liabilities are in practice due on demand; the assets are long-term. The current mortgages were mostly issued when inflation, and therefore interest rates, were much lower than they are now. If the mortgages were revalued at current yields, that is, at the market prices for which they could be sold in a free secondary market, virtually every U.S. savings and loan association would be technically insolvent.

So long as the thrift institutions can maintain their level of deposits, no problem arises because they do not have to liquidate their assets. But if inflation speeds up, interest rates on market instruments will rise further. Unless the thrift institutions offer competitive interest rates, their shareholders or depositors will withdraw funds to get a better yield (the process inelegantly termed "disintermediation"). But with their income fixed, the thrift institutions will find it difficult or impossible to pay competitive rates. This situation is concealed but not altered by the legal limits on the rates they are permitted to pay.

Further acceleration of inflation threatens a major crisis for this group of financial institutions. And the crisis is no minor matter. Total assets of these U.S. institutions approach $400 billion. As it happens, they would be greatly helped by a deceleration of inflation, but some of their recent borrowers who are locked into high rates on mortgages would be seriously hurt.

Benefits of inflation-proofed loans. Consider how different the situation of the thrift institutions would be with widespread escalator clauses: The mortgages on their books would be yielding, say, 5 percent plus the rate of inflation; they could afford to pay to their shareholders or depositors, say, 3 or 4 percent plus the rate of inflation. They, their borrowers, and their shareholders or depositors would be fully protected against changes in the rate of inflation. They would be assuming risks only with respect to the much smaller possible changes in the *real* rate of interest rather than in the money rate.

Similarly an insurance company could afford to offer an inflation-protected policy if its assets were in inflation-protected loans to business or in mortgages or government securities. A pension fund could offer inflation-protected pensions if it held inflation-protected assets. In Brazil, where this practice has, to my knowledge, been carried furthest, banks are required to credit a "monetary correction" equal to the rate of inflation on all time deposits and to charge a "monetary correction" on all loans extending beyond some minimum period.

To repeat, none of these arrangements is without cost. It would be far better if stable prices made them unnecessary. But they seem to me far less costly than continuing on the road to periodic acceleration of inflation, ending in a real bust.

The suggested governmental arrangements would stimulate the private arrangements. Today, one deterrent to issuing private purchasing-power securities is that the inflation adjustment would be taxable to the recipient along with the real interest paid. The proposed tax changes would in effect exempt such adjustments from taxation, and so make purchasing-power securities more attractive to lenders. In addition, government issues of purchasing-power securities would offer effective competition to private borrowers, inducing them to follow suit, and would provide assets that could be used as the counterpart of inflation-protected liabilities.

Prospects for private contract escalators. Will escalator clauses spread in private contracts? That depends on the course of inflation. If, by some miracle, inflation were to disappear in the near future, all talk of such arrangements would also disappear. The more likely development is that U.S. inflation will taper off in late 1974, will settle at something like 6 or 7 percent in 1975, and will then start to accelerate in 1976 in response to the delayed impact of overreaction in 1974 to rising unemployment. During this period there will be a steady but unspectacular expansion of escalator clauses. If inflation accelerates to 10 percent and beyond in 1977 or so, the steady expansion will turn into a bandwagon.

Needless to say, I hope this scenario is wrong. I hope that the Federal Reserve and the Administration will be willing and able to resist the pressure to overreact to the 1974 recession, that they will maintain fiscal and monetary restraint and so avoid another acceleration of inflation. But neither past experience nor the present political climate makes that hope a reasonable expectation.

42

Making it easier to fight inflation. How would widespread adoption of the escalator principle affect economic policy? Some critics say indexation would condemn us to perpetual inflation. I believe that, on the contrary, indexation would enhance government's ability to act against inflation.

To begin with, indexation will temper some of the hardships and distortions that now follow from a drop in the rate of inflation. Employers will not be stuck with excessively high wage increases under existing union contracts, for wage increases will moderate as inflation recedes. Borrowers will not be stuck with excessively high interest costs, for the rates on outstanding loans will moderate as inflation recedes. Indexation will also partly counteract the tendency of businesses to defer capital investment once total spending begins to decline, for there will be less reason to wait in expectation of lower prices and lower interest rates. Businesses will be able to borrow funds or enter into construction contracts knowing that interest rates and contract prices will be adjusted later in accord with indexes of prices.

Most important, indexation will shorten the time it takes for a reduction in the rate of growth of total spending to have its full effect in reducing the rate of inflation. As the deceleration of demand pinches at various points in the economy, any effects on prices will be transmitted promptly to wage contracts, contracts for future delivery, and interest rates on outstanding long-term loans. Accordingly, producers' wage costs and other costs will go up less rapidly than they would without indexation. This tempering of costs, in turn, will encourage employers to keep more people on the payroll and to produce more goods than they would without indexation. The encouragement of supply, in turn, will work against price increases, with additional moderating feedback on wages and other costs.

With widespread indexation, in sum, firm monetary restraint by the Federal Reserve System (the "Fed") would be reflected in a much more even reduction in the pace of inflation and a much smaller transitory rise in unemployment. The success in slowing inflation would steel political will to suffer the smaller withdrawal pains and so might make it possible for the "Fed" to persist in a firm policy. As it became credible that the "Fed" would persist, private reactions could reinforce the effects of its policy. The economy would move to noninflationary growth at high levels of employment much more rapidly than now seems possible.

6. Objections to Escalator Clauses

The major objection to widespread escalation is the allegation that escalators have an inflationary impact on the economy. In this simple-minded form, the statement is simply false—as I noted earlier in connection with the 1970 General Motors settlement. An escalator goes into effect only as the *result* of a *previous* price increase. Whence came that? An escalator can go down as well as up. If inflation slows, and hence so do wage increases, do escalators have a *deflationary* impact?

In the first instance, escalators have *no* direct effect on the rate of inflation. They simply ensure that inflation affects different prices and wages alike and thus avoid the kind of distortions in relative prices and wages illustrated by the General Motors case. With widespread escalation, inflation would be *transmitted* more quickly and evenly, and hence the harm done by inflation would be less. But why should that raise or lower the *rate* of inflation?

Incentive to raise inflation tax rate? Two objections have been made on a more sophisticated level. First, widespread escalation would restrict the government revenue from inflation simply to the direct tax on cash balances produced by the issue of additional high-powered money (point (1), page 29). It would thereby reduce the revenue from a given rate of inflation, which could induce government to raise the rate of tax.

Second, the general public could interpret the adoption of escalator clauses as demonstrating that the government has given up the fight against inflation and is seeking only to "live with inflation." This might lead the public to raise its own anticipations of future inflation, which, by reducing its willingness to hold cash balances, could cause a once-for-all rise in the price level and to that extent be a self-fulfilling prophecy.

Neither objection seems to me weighty. If the public does not wish to stop inflation but is content to allow government to use inflation as a regular source of revenue, the sooner we adapt our institutions to that situation the better. Similarly, the second objection has little relevance to the proposal for escalator clauses as a means for removing *political* obstacles to ending inflation.

On a still more sophisticated level, it can be argued that, by removing distortions in relative prices produced by inflation, widespread escalator clauses would make it easier for the public to recognize changes in the rate of inflation, would thereby reduce the time-lag in adapting to such changes, and thus make the nominal price level more sensitive and variable. This is certainly possible, though by no means demonstrated. But, if so, the *real variables* would be made *less* sensitive and *more* stable—a highly beneficial trade off. Moreover, it is also possible that, by making accurate estimates of the rate of inflation less important, widespread escalator clauses would reduce the attention devoted to such estimates, and thereby provide more stability.

An objection of a very different kind is that inflation serves the critical social purpose of resolving incompatible demands by different groups. To put it crudely, the participants in the economy have "nonnegotiable demands" for more than the whole output. These demands are reconciled because inflation fools people into believing that their demands have been met when in fact they have not been, nominal returns being eroded by unanticipated inflation.

Escalator clauses, it is argued, bring the inconsistent demands into the open. Workers who would accept a lower real wage produced by unanticipated inflation will not be willing to accept the same real wage in explicit negotiations. If this view is correct on a wide enough scale to be important, I see no ultimate outcome other than either runaway inflation or an authoritarian society ruled by force. Perhaps it is only wishful thinking that makes me reluctant to accept this vision of our fate.

Conclusion

The conventional political wisdom is that the citizenry may mutter about inflation but votes on the basis of the level of unemployment. Nobody, it is said, has ever lost an election because of inflation, but Hoover in 1932 and Nixon in 1960 lost because of unemployment.

As we leave the depression decade farther and farther behind, and as we experience more and more inflation, this conventional wisdom becomes increasingly questionable. Inflation surely helped to make Edward Heath prime minister in 1970 and, even more surely, ex-prime minister in 1974. The popularity of Japan's prime minister, K. Tanaka, is at an all-time low because of inflation. President Allende of Chile lost his life at least partly because of inflation. Throughout the world, inflation is a major source of political unrest.

Perhaps widespread escalator clauses are not the best expedient in this time of trouble. But I know of no other that has been suggested that holds out as much promise of both reducing the harm done by inflation and facilitating the ending of inflation. If inflation continues to accelerate, the conventional political wisdom will be reversed. The insistence on ending inflation at whatever cost will lead to a severe depression. Now, before that has occurred, is the time to take measures that will make it politically feasible to end inflation before inflation ends not only the conventional wisdom but perhaps also the free society.

Appendix A: A Classical Forerunner—Alfred Marshall

1. On the "Tabular Standard " *

I agree with the general opinion that a steady upward tendency in general prices conduces a little more to the general well-being than does a tendency downwards, because it keeps industry somewhat better employed. But, on the other hand, people of all classes, and especially of the working classes, spend their incomes more wisely when prices and money-wages are falling, and they think themselves worse off than they are, than when a rise of prices and money-wages leads them to exaggerate their real incomes and to be careless about their expenditure. So that, on the whole, I think there is much less difference than is generally supposed between the net benefits of periods of rising and falling prices. It is doubtful whether the last ten years, which are regarded as years of depression, but in which there have been few violent movements of prices, have not, on the whole, conduced more to solid progress and true happiness than the alternations of feverish activity and painful retrogression which have characterised every preceding decade of this century. In fact, I regard violent fluctuations of prices as a much greater evil than a gradual fall of prices. I will venture to quote a passage from a paper on remedies for the discontinuity of industry, which I read last year at the "Industrial Remuneration Conference":

> A great cause of the discontinuity of industry is the want of certain knowledge as to what a pound is going to be worth a short time hence. With every expansion and contraction of credit prices rise and fall. This change of prices presses heavily even on those who kept themselves as far as possible from the uncertainties of trade, and increases in many ways the intensity of commercial fluctuations. For just when private traders and public companies are most inclined to reckless ventures, the interest which they have to

---

* Excerpt from "Reply to the Royal Commission on the Depression of Trade and Industry" (1886), reproduced in *Official Papers by Alfred Marshall* (London: Macmillan, 1926).

pay on borrowed capital represents an exceptionally small purchasing power, because prices are high. And in the opposite phase, when their resources are crippled by the stagnation of business the lowness of prices compels them to sacrifice a much greater amount of real wealth in order to pay their interest. When traders are rejoicing in high prices debenture and mortgage holders and other creditors are depressed; and when the pendulum swings the other way traders, already depressed, are kept under water by having to pay an exceptionally heavy toll to their creditors. This serious evil can be much diminished by a plan which economists have long advocated. In proposing this remedy I want Government to help business, though not to do business. It should publish tables showing as closely as may be the changes in the purchasing power of gold, and should facilitate contracts for payments to be made in terms of units of fixed purchasing power.

Government already does work of the kind desired in regard to the tithe commutation tables. But instead of dealing with wheat, barley, and oats, it would deal with all important commodities. It would publish their prices once a month or once a year; it would reckon the importance of each commodity as proportioned to the total sum spent on it, and then by simple arithmetic deduce the change in the purchasing power of gold. Borrowings could then, at the option of the contracting parties, be reckoned in Government units. On this plan, if A lends B 1,000*l.* at 4½ percent interest, and after some years the purchasing power of money had risen by an eighth, B would have to pay as interest, not 45*l.*, but a sum that had the same purchasing power as 45*l.* had at the time of borrowing, i.e. 40*l.*, and so on. The plan would have to win its way into general use, but when once it had become familiar none but gamblers would lend or borrow on any other terms, at all events for long periods. The scheme has no claims to theoretic perfection, but only to being a great improvement on our present methods, and obtained with little trouble. A perfectly exact measure of purchasing power is not only unattainable, but even unthinkable. The same change of prices affects the purchasing power of money to different persons in different ways. For to him who can seldom afford to have meat, a fall of one-fourth in the price of meat accompanied by a rise of one-fourth in that of bread means a fall in the purchasing power of money; his wages will not go so far as before. While to his richer neighbor, who spends twice as much on meat as on bread, the change acts the other way. The Government would, of course, take account only of the total consumption of the whole nation; but even so it would be troubled by constant changes in the way in which the nation spent its income. The estimate of the importance of different commodities would have to be recast from time to time. The only room for differences of opinion would be as to what commodities should be taken account of. It would probably be best to follow the ordinary method of taking very little account of any but raw commodities. Manufactured commodities and personal services are always changing their character, and are not easily priced. Manufactured tend to fall in value relatively to raw commodities, and at present, at all events, personal services tend to rise, so that the errors made by omitting both probably nearly neutralises one another. Simplicity and definiteness are in this case far more important than theoretic accuracy. Those who make the returns should work in the open day, so that they could not, if they would, be subject to many influences. This plan, though strange at first sight, would really be much simpler than bimetallism, while its influence in steadying industry would be incomparably greater.

The task of publishing from time to time the currency value of a unit of constant purchasing power cannot, I think, be performed properly except by a permanent Government department. So far as the exports and imports go, the materials for this have been provided by the Board of Trade. Their work is a perfect model of method, which cannot fail to be of use to us; but it is not directly applicable to our present purpose. In Mr. Palgrave's memorandum a most interesting example is shown of the kind of index-number that is wanted. But Government alone can command the machinery requisite to secure properly tested figures for the purpose.

The unit of constant general purchasing power would be applicable, at the free choice of both parties concerned, for nearly all contracts for the payment of interest, and for the repayment of loans; and for many contracts for rent, and for wages and salaries. But as people became more familiar with the plan, certain modifications might gradually be made, again by the consent of those concerned, for special cases. For instance, there might be an agricultural unit, either suggested directly by the Government or adapted by private persons from the figures supplied by the Government. This unit would be got from the general unit by increasing the weight of the prices of agricultural produce. It might be agreed that while the total amounts spent on other things should be taken as they are, every 1,000,000*l.* spent on agricultural produce should be treated for this

48

special purpose as though it were (say) 4,000,000*l*. This plan would, I think, be fairer, and, when once thoroughly understood, more popular, than the plan which has been proposed of fixing agricultural rents at the price of a certain amount of farm produce. Again, by a similar modification, a mining unit might be got which would supersede the useful but not quite satisfactory sliding scales that are adopted at present; and so for other trades.

I wish to emphasise the fact that this proposal is independent of the form of our currency, and does not ask for any change in it. I admit that the plan would seldom be available for the purposes of international trade. But its importance as a steadying influence to our home trade would be so great, and its introduction would be so easy and so free from the evils which generally surround the interference of Government in business, that I venture to urge strongly its claims on your immediate attention. . . .

2. On a Standard of Value Independent of Gold and Silver **

. . . Leaving some difficulties of detail to be discussed at the end of the article, let us suppose that (as was suggested long ago by Joseph Lowe, Poulett Scrope and others)[1] a Government Department extends to all commodities the action taken by the Commissioners of Tithes with regard to wheat, barley and oats. As they, having ascertained the average prices of grain at any time, state how much money is required to purchase as much wheat, barley and oats as would have cost £100 at certain standard prices, so this Department, having ascertained the prices of all important commodities, would publish from time to time the amount of money required to give the same general purchasing power, as, say, £1 had at the beginning of 1887. The prices used by it would be the latest attainable; not, as in the case of tithes, the mean of the prices for the last seven years. This standard unit of purchasing power might be called for shortness simply *The Unit*.

From time to time, at the beginning of each year or oftener, the Department would declare how much of the currency had the same purchasing power as £1 had at the beginning of 1887. If, for instance, it declared in 1890 that 18s. had this purchasing power, then a contract to pay a unit in 1890 would be discharged by paying 18s.

** Excerpt from "Remedies for Fluctuations of General Prices" (1887), *Memorials of Alfred Marshall*, ed. A. C. Pigou (London: Macmillan, 1925), pp. 197–199.

[1] Some account of their suggestions is given in the chapter on "A Tabular Standard of Value" in Jevons's *Money*.

If it declared in 1892 that 23s. had only the same purchasing power as £1 had in 1887, or 18s. in 1890, then any contract to pay a unit in 1892 would require for its settlement the delivery of 23s.

When a loan was made, it could, at the option of those concerned, be made in terms of currency, or in terms of units. In the latter case the lender would know that whatever change there might be in the value of money, he would receive when the debt was repaid just the same amount of real wealth, just the same command over the necessaries, comforts and luxuries of life as he had lent away. If he bargained for 5 per cent interest, he would each year receive money equal in value to one-twentieth of the units which he had lent; and however prices might have changed, these would contribute a certain and definite amount to his real means of expenditure. The borrower would not be at one time impatient to start ill-considered enterprises in order to gain by the expected rise in general prices, and at another afraid of borrowing for legitimate business for fear of being caught by a general fall in prices.

Of course every trade would still have its own dangers due to causes peculiar to itself; but by the use of the unit it might avoid those heavy risks which are caused by a rise or fall in general prices. Salaries and wages, where not determined by special sliding scales, could be fixed in units, their real value would then no longer fluctuate constantly in the wrong direction, tending upwards just when, if it changed at all, it should fall, and tending downwards just when, if it changed at all, it should rise.[2]

Ground-rents also should be fixed in general units, though for agricultural rents it would be best to have a special unit based chiefly on the prices of farm produce. The reckoning of mortgages and marriage settlements in terms of units of purchasing power, instead of gold, would remove one great source of uncertainty from the affairs of private life, while a similar change as to debentures and Government bonds would give the holders of them what they want— a really constant income. The ordinary shareholders in a public company would no longer be led to take an over-sanguine estimate of their position by a period of prosperity, which, besides enriching them directly, diminished the real payments which they have to make

---

[2] Sliding scales, admirable as is their general effect, perhaps err by being too simple. A sliding scale in the iron trade, for instance, should, I think, take account not only of the price of the finished iron, but also, on the one hand, of the prices of iron ore, coal, and other expenses of the employer, and, on the other, of the prices of the things chiefly consumed by the workmen. Trades in which sliding scales are possible could arrange special units for themselves, by aid of the statistics on which Government would base its general unit.

to debenture holders and perhaps to preference stock holders. And, on the other hand, they would not be oppressed by the extra weight of having to pay more than their real value on account of these fixed charges when prices were low and business drooping.

The standard unit of purchasing power being published, the Law Courts should, I think, give every facility to contracts, wills, and other documents made in terms of the unit; and Government itself might gradually feel its way towards assessing rates and taxes (except, of course, such things as payments for postage stamps) in terms of the unit, and also towards reckoning the salaries, pensions, and, when possible, the wages of its employees at so many units instead of so much currency. It should, I think, begin by offering, as soon as the unit was made, to pay for each £100 of Consols a really uniform interest of three units, instead of a nominally uniform but really fluctuating interest of £3. The public, though at first regarding the new notion as uncanny, would, I believe, take to it rapidly as soon as they got to see its substantial advantages. Their dislike of it even at first would be less than was their dislike of coal fires, of railways, and of gas. Ere long the currency would, I believe, be restricted to the functions for which it is well fitted, of measuring and settling transactions that are completed shortly after they are begun. I think we ought, without delay, to set about preparing for voluntary use an authoritative unit; being voluntary it would be introduced tentatively, and would be a powerful remedy for a great evil. This plan would not cause any forced disturbance of existing contracts, such as would result from a change of our currency. It would give a better standard for deferred payments than could possibly be given by a currency (as ordinarily understood), and therefore would diminish the temptation to hurry on impetuously a change of our currency with the object of making its value a little more stable; and it could be worked equally well with any currency. . . .

Appendix B: English Classical Political Economy and the Debate on Indexation *

The question of whether, and how, a country's legal standard of value should be adjusted to correct for the distortion created by rising or falling prices seems to have been discussed by nineteenth-century writers following periods of fairly substantial inflation and deflation. The Napoleonic Wars and the aftermath was a period of

* This appendix was prepared by Brian Griffiths.

fairly rapid inflation followed by a rather sharp deflation; between 1792 and 1814 prices rose by just over 60 percent, between 1814 and 1822 they fell by 40 percent. At least three writers in the 1820s and 1830s, Joseph Lowe, G. Poulett Scrope and G. R. Porter, analyzed the effects of inflation and proposed correcting the standard of value for changes in the cost of living. They set out to show that in the first place it was possible to construct an index of consumer prices. Lowe proposed that the prices of staple articles of household consumption should be collected regularly and that a "table of reference" should be framed showing the weighting attached to various commodities. Although Porter produced a table showing the average monthly fluctuations of 50 leading commodities between 1833 and 1837, none of the three attempted to work out the details of how such an index might be constructed.

Joseph Lowe. Of the three studies, by far the best is Joseph Lowe's *The Present State of England in Regard to Agriculture, Trade and Finance, with a Comparison of the Prospects of England and France* (1822). Both the purpose and general outline of his scheme are very clear:

> a table exhibiting from year to year, the power of money in purchase would give to annuitants and other contracting parties, the means of maintaining an agreement, not in its letter only, but in its spirit; of conferring on a specified sum a uniformity and permanency of value, by *changing the numerical value in proportion of the change in its power of purchase.*

Such an adjustment might be made every three, five or seven years.

Lowe was particularly perceptive in his analysis of the beneficial effects of such a scheme on agriculture, the labor market, and the national debt. Because of uncertainty about the value of money, landlords are reluctant to agree to long leases during periods of inflation while tenants are reluctant to accept such leases during periods of deflation. The effect is that rents tend to be fixed in terms of the price of corn or that the land is not leased at all. Both results are harmful. If, however, the money value of rent were to be corrected for inflation, the problems would not arise and agriculture would maintain its prosperity.

His description of the labor market seems remarkably prescient. He claimed that the previous thirty years had been a time of frequent contention between employer and employed, and that wages in the metropolis were sticky in a downward direction, with real wages being too high during the period of deflation.

Wages, salaries, professional fees are almost all on as high a scale as during the war, notwithstanding the cessation of the two great causes of the rise—the expense of living and the extra demand for labour. The persons whether of high or low station, who are in receipt of the established allowance if called on for an abatement, would naturally plead the uncertainty of provisions continuing at their present rate; and nothing it is evident will induce them willingly to assent to a reduction, except a guarantee against a recurrence of the grand evil—a rise in prices. In this most desirable object we should hope to succeed, not by a compulsory course, not by an interference between the payer and the receiver, but by an alternative offered to their voluntary adoption by putting it in their power, when making a time contract, to give a permanent value to a money stipulation, or to find when no such precaution was taken, an equitable standard of reference.
Such a regulator would carry conviction to all parties and operate greatly to abridge altercation. At a time like the present it would relieve the inferior from much of the anxiety and humiliation attendant on reduction; and in the case of a rise in prices it would guide the employer to a fairer advance of wages, the distributor of charitable aid to a fair apportionment of relief.

Although he did not venture into details of how the value of government bonds would be adjusted for inflation, he seems to have suggested that the price of the stock would rise *pari passu* with the index of inflation, as would the income from bonds. Therefore, no matter "whether the country was at peace or war; whether its currency were sound or depreciated; whether the mines of gold and silver throughout the world became more or less productive" we should be assured of "a permanent value to our public dividends."
As a precedent Lowe mentioned the Court of Teinds and the tithe of Scotland. The court decided that clerical income should be regulated by the price of corn in the public market over a series of years. In conclusion he asked why such a scheme had not been adopted. His answer was twofold: "the unfortunate neglect of political economy in the education of our public men; and the interest of government, the greatest of all debtors, to allow money to undergo a gradual depreciation."

W. Stanley Jevons. In his book *Money and the Mechanisms of Exchange* (1875), W. Stanley Jevons argued very forcefully for a better standard of value.

> The question thus arises whether the progress of economical and statistical science might not enable us to devise some better standard of value. We have seen (pp. 136–143) that the so-called double standard system of money spreads the fluctuations of supply and demand of gold and silver over a larger area, and maintains both metals more unchanged in value than they would otherwise be. Can we not conceive a multiple legal tender, which would be still less liable to variation? We estimate the value of one hundred pounds by the quantities of corn, beef, potatoes, coal, timber, iron, tea, coffee, beer, and other principal commodities, which it will purchase from time to time. Might we not invent a legal tender note which should be convertible, not into any one single commodity, but into an aggregate of small quantities of various commodities, the quantity and quality of each being rigorously defined? Thus a hundred pound note would give the owners a right to demand one quarter of good wheat, one ton of ordinary merchant bar iron, one hundred pounds weight of middling cotton, twenty pounds of sugar, five pounds of tea, and other articles sufficient to make up the value. All these commodities will, of course, fluctuate in their relative values, but if the holder of the note loses upon some, he will in all probability gain upon others, so that on the average his note will remain steady in purchasing power. Indeed, as the articles into which it is convertible are those needed for continual consumption, the purchasing power of the note must remain steady compared with that of gold or silver, which metals are employed only for a few special purposes.

Although such a currency would be impracticable, because no one wished to have all the articles included in the standard, he proposed the creation of a "tabular standard of value," changes of which would be used to adjust the value of contracts fixed in money terms. He suggested that, to implement such a proposal, a permanent government commission would have to be created and endowed with a kind of judicial power. The officers of the commission would collect current commodity prices "in all the principal markets of the kingdom" and then compute the average variations in the purchasing power of gold. The decisions of the commission would be published monthly and payments for wages, rents, annuities, et cetera, would be adjusted in accordance with them; at first the scheme would be entirely voluntary, but then after its undoubted value had been shown it would be made compulsory for every debt over three months.

The scheme Jevons suggested had many advantages: it would result in a whole new degree of stability in social relations; it would guarantee the fixed incomes of individuals and public institutions; speculation would be discouraged; the calculations of merchants would be less frequently frustrated by causes beyond their own control; and many bankruptcies would be averted, as the intensity of crises was lessened, because as prices fell, the liabilities of debtors would decrease proportionately. The only real difficulty Jevons saw with such a scheme was the method by which changes in the purchasing power of gold were to be calculated.

Walter Bagehot. Bagehot thought differently. In an article in the *Economist* (20 November 1875), he raised four objections to Jevons's proposal. First, it would be wholly unfit for a country with foreign trade. It would discourage trade because of the increased uncertainty in exchanging currency for gold. London had developed as a financial center because of the stability of its standard and this was one way to wreck it. Secondly, it would make banking impossible, as a banker would never know what he owed; each debt, being contracted at a different time, would have an uncertain value. Thirdly, Bagehot foresaw severe difficulties in calculating the index, especially in maintaining a constant quality for the articles included. Lastly, in a good currency the paying medium ought either to be identical with, or readily interchangeable into, a definite quantity of the standard of value. But in the Jevons proposal, the standard was fixed while the paying medium was in a state of incessant fluctuation. For these reasons Bagehot felt that "we must adhere to one or other of the precious metals as a standard of value, like our forefathers."

Robert Giffen. In an article in the *Economic Journal* for 1892 entitled "Fancy Monetary Standards," which is a reply to an article in the previous issue by Aneurin Williams entitled "A Value of Bullion Standard" (a proposal to provide for an issue of paper which was to consist of promises to pay a varying quantity of bullion, the variation depending on the change in a specified index number), Robert Giffen restated Bagehot's objections—concluding that they were "altogether so destructive as to make it unnecessary to go farther," but nevertheless adding some of his own. Firstly, he argued that monetary standards should not be changed unless the reasons were overwhelming. Because good money was so very difficult to get and most governments, when they meddled with money, were apt to make great blunders, the standard for money was best left alone. Secondly, he claimed that the proposal would only be feasible with an inconvertible and managed paper. Thirdly, there was the problem of actually constructing the index. Lastly, the problem of adjusting wages over short periods to changes in the index would give rise to difficulties in the labor market.

Alfred Marshall. Alfred Marshall's proposals for establishing a unit of constant general purchasing power were set out in a paper read at the Industrial Remuneration Conference in 1885. This paper was subsequently included in his answers to questions put by the Royal Commission on the Depression of Trade and Industry (1886) and in an article published in the *Contemporary Review* for March 1887, which was included in a memorandum submitted by him to the Royal Commission on the Values of Gold and Silver (1887, 1888), parts of which are reproduced in Appendix A. Unlike that of Jevons's multiple legal standard, the essence of his plan was not to change the form of the currency but to adjust the value of all contracts fixed in money terms for changes in the average price level. He also put forward a proposal for changing the form of the currency so as to make it a true bimetallic standard, but he was very careful to separate the two schemes, and also to warn against the possible dangers of changing the base of the currency.

In an exchange of letters with Professor Irving Fisher in 1911 and 1912, Marshall remained convinced of the value of the proposals which he put forward twenty-five years earlier.

> But a quarter of a century has made me ever more desirous that every country should have an official "unit" of general purchasing power, made up from tables of price percentages like those of Sauerbeck and others: and that it should authorise long-period obligations for the payment of rent and interest on loans of all kinds to be made at the option of the contracting parties, in terms either of this general unit, or of a selection of price percentages appropriate to the special purpose in hand. Public authority should make out such lists as appeared suitable to particular classes of transactions: but the parties concerned should have perfect freedom to make special selections. Any wages contract, such as a sliding scale in the iron trade, might "take account not only of the price of the finished iron, but also on the one hand, of the prices of iron ore, coal, and other expenses of the employer; and on the other, of the price of the things chiefly consumed by the workmen.

I think that could be done at once. If it succeeded, the world would, I think, be prepared in say twenty years for an international "fixed standard" paper currency, provided that it can be helped on the way by a vigorous movement such as that in which you are active. [16 September 1911]

In a third letter to Fisher, he throws some light on Giffen's earlier article and his own doubts about the scheme.

When Giffen uttered his vehement trumpet blast against "Fancy Monetary Standards" I chaffed him about his energy, and I recollect that he said that his argument was not opposed to my scheme. Recollecting that just now, I further remember that my doubt about the practicability of my original scheme was connected with International Stock Exchange Securities bearing a fixed rate of interest (among other things). [15 October 1912]

J. M. Keynes. Recalling Marshall's proposals of the 1880s, J. M. Keynes, one of Marshall's great admirers, recommended to the Royal Commission on National Debt and Taxation (1927) in 1924 that the government should issue an index-linked bond, claiming that the advantages of such a scheme were even greater than in the 1880s.

I suggest that there is one further type of bond not yet in issue which might prove popular with particular individuals and so enable the State to raise funds a little more cheaply. I suggest that there should be issued bonds of which the capital and the interest would be paid not in a fixed amount of sterling, but in such amount of sterling as has a fixed commodity value as indicated by an index number. I think that an official index number should be established for such purposes on the lines of the optional tabular standard recommended long ago by Dr. Marshall, and that it should be open to anyone, including particularly the Treasury, to offer loans, the payment of the interest on which and the repayment of the capital of which would be governed by movements of the index number. I can say from knowledge that there are many investors, who, wishing to take no risks would naturally confine themselves to trustee stocks, yet feel a natural anxiety in being compelled to invest their whole resources in terms of legal tender money, the relation of which to real value has been shown by experience to be variable. Throughout almost the whole of Europe investors of the trustee type have been deprived in the past ten years of the greater part of the value of their property. Even here in England all such investors have suffered a very large real loss. We may hope that great instability in the value of the currency may not be one of the things which the future has in store for us. But it is natural that some people should be anxious about it. Unless, therefore, the Treasury hopes to make a profit through the depreciation of legal tender, it would lose nothing, and might gain something in terms of interest, by issuing such bonds as I have indicated.

Otto Niemeyer. The Commission raised the practicability of such a proposal with Sir Otto E. Niemeyer, controller of finance at the Treasury. His opinion of the scheme was that he did "not quite see why it should attract anybody" and that although some investors did take such a "long and elaborate view," for ordinary people "this would be too clever altogether." For Sir Otto such a proposal was connected with countries which had experienced great changes in the value of money such as Germany, which was not the expectation of the U.K. In any case, when the Treasury had issued five- to fifteen-year bonds, the interest on which varied according to Treasury bill rate, which he claimed was similar to Keynes's proposal, they were not a success. He was of the opinion that before the state issued such a bond he would like to see it tried in practice by a private person, such as one of the more enterprising insurance companies.

Appendix C: A Bibliography

1. EARLY CONTROVERSY

Lowe, Joseph. *The Present State of England in Regard to Agriculture, Trade, and Finance, with a Comparison of the Prospects of England and France.* London, 1822.

Scrope, G. Poulett. *An Examination of the Bank Charter Question with an Inquiry into the Nature of a Just Standard of Value.* London, 1833.

Porter, G. R. *Principles of Political Economy.* London, 1833.

——. *Political Economy for Plain People.* London, 1833.

——. *The Progress of the Nation.* London, 1838.

Jevons, W. S. (1875). "A Tabular Standard of Value." Chapter 25 of *Money and the Mechanism of Exchange.* New York, 1898, pp. 318–326.

Bagehot, Walter (1875). "A New Standard of Value." *Economist,* London, 20 November 1875. Reprinted in *Economic Journal,* London, vol. 2 (1892), pp. 472–477.

Giffen, R. (1892). "Fancy Monetary Standards." *Economic Journal,* London, vol. 2 (1892), pp. 463–471.

Marshall, Alfred (1886). "Reply to the Royal Commission on the Depression of Trade and Industry." Reproduced in *Official Papers by Alfred Marshall.* London: Macmillan, 1926, pp. 9–12.

————. (1887). Article in *Contemporary Review,* March 1887. Reproduced in *Memorials of Alfred Marshall.* Edited by A. C. Pigou. London: Macmillan, 1925, pp. 188–211.

————. (1911). Letter to Irving Fisher. Reproduced in *Memorials of Alfred Marshall,* p. 476.

Keynes, J. M. (1927). Evidence Presented to the Committee on National Debt and Taxation. In *Minutes of Evidence* (Colwyn Committee). London: HMSO, 1927. Vol. 1, p. 278 and p. 287.

Niemeyer, Sir Otto (1927). Dismissal of Keynes's Proposal (as above), *Minutes of Evidence,* vol. 2, p. 633.

"Agenda for the Age of Inflation—II." *Economist,* 25 August 1951, pp. 435–437.

2. OFFICIAL REPORTS

United Kingdom

Committee on the Working of the Monetary System (Radcliffe Committee, August 1959). *Report.* Cmnd. 827. London: HMSO, 1959, pp. 211-212.

————. *Memoranda of Evidence.* Vol. 3, part 13, no. 6, pp. 66–69.

————. *Minutes of Evidence.* Qq. 10,043-10,141, pp. 663–664.

Committee to Review National Savings (Page Committee, June 1973). *Report.* Cmnd. 5273. London: HMSO, pp. 190–198, 309–314.

United States

Joint Committee on the Economic Report. *Monetary Policy and the Management of the Public Debt.* 82d Congress, 2d session, Washington, 1952.

Friedman, Milton, and Machlup, Fritz. Before the Patman Subcommittee. In Joint Committee on the Economic Report. *Monetary Policy and the Management of the Public Debt,* pp. 1105–1106.

Replies of Treasury and Council of Economic Advisers. In Joint Committee on the Economic Report. *Monetary Policy and the Management of the Public Debt,* pp. 142-145, 888-889.

Tobin, James. "An Essay on Principles of Debt Management." In Commission on Money and Credit. *Fiscal and Debt Management Policies.* Englewood Cliffs, N.J.: Prentice-Hall, 1963, pp. 202–213.

Holzman, F. D. "Escalation and Its Use to Mitigate the Inequities of Inflation." In Commission on Money and Credit. *Inflation, Growth and Employment.* Englewood Cliffs, N.J.: Prentice-Hall, 1964.

3. INTERNATIONAL AGENCIES

Finch, David. "Purchasing Power Guarantees for Deferred Payments." *IMF Staff Papers*, February 1956, pp. 1–22.

OECD. Committee for Invisible Transactions. *Formation of Savings.* Capital Market Study, vol. 2. Paris, 1968, pp. 39–41, 97–105, 139–140, 176, 194.

Lall, S. "Countering Inflation: the Role of Value Linking." *Finance and Development*, June 1969, pp. 10–15.

Liefmann-Keil, Elizabeth. "Index-based Adjustments for Social Security Benefits." *International Labour Review*, May 1959, pp. 487–510.

OECD. Committee on Financial Markets. *Indexation of Fixed-Interest Securities.* Paris, 1974.

UN. "Index Clauses in Deferred Payments." *Economic Bulletin for Latin America*, October 1957, pp. 73–89.

4. ACADEMIC PAPERS

Hein, J. "A Note on the Use of Index Clauses Abroad." *Journal of Finance*, December 1960, pp. 546–552.

Arvidsson, G. "Should We Have Indexed Loans?" In *Inflation.* Edited by D. C. Hague. New York, 1962, pp. 112–126.

———. "Reflections on Index Loans." *Skandinoviska Banken Quarterly Review*, 1959–60, pp. 1–14.

Morag, Amotz. "For an Inflation-proof Economy." *American Economic Review*, March 1962, pp. 177–185.

Eagly, Robert. "An Interpretation of Palander's Twin Securities Markets Proposal." *Southern Economic Journal*, July 1960, pp. 51–54.

———. "On Government Issuance of an Index Bond." *Public Finance*, no. 3 (1967), pp. 268–284.

Bach, G. L., and Musgrave, R. A. "A Stable Purchasing Power Bond." *American Economic Review*, December 1941, pp. 823–825.

Cohen, B. I. "The Use of Indexed Debts in Underdeveloped Countries." *Public Finance*, no. 4 (1966), pp. 441–457.

Goode, Richard. "A Constant Purchasing-Power Savings Bond." *National Tax Journal*, vol. 4 (1951), pp. 332–340.

Sarnat, Marshall. "Purchasing Power Risk, Portfolio Analysis, and the Case for Index-Linked Bonds." *Journal of Money, Credit and Banking*, August 1973, pp. 836–845.

Robson, Peter. "Index-Linked Bonds." *Review of Economic Studies*, October 1960, pp. 57–68.

———. "Inflation-Proof Loans." *National Westminster Bank Quarterly Review*, May 1974, pp. 48–60.

3
THE CONTROVERSIAL ISSUE OF COMPREHENSIVE INDEXATION
William Fellner

The Nature of the Current Debate

The usual argument for comprehensive indexation implies assumptions which I consider unrealistic. To my knowledge no contributor to the professional debate has suggested that indexation—and the periodic revisions of payment obligations that it entails—would provide adequate protection against the harmful effects of accelerating inflation on resource allocation and on welfare in general. The proponents of comprehensive indexation usually do argue, however, that the system would make it easier to get inflation under control.

It is sometimes implied that a government which is relying on inflation to divert output away from the private economy will stop applying this kind of hidden taxation if, in consequence of the rapid and automatic wage-price revisions occurring under indexation, any given degree of inflation becomes a less effective means of diverting resources. I think the contrary is much more likely to be true: a government engaged in this kind of hidden taxation is much more apt to step up its inflationary moves than to abandon them, if more money is needed to achieve the same result in real terms.

However, we should pay attention not merely to cases in which the authorities "initiate" inflation in order to acquire resources without taxation but also (and, at present, perhaps mainly) to cases in which the authorities are known to "accommodate" steep cost trends at high levels of resource utilization for fear that failure to do so would lead to a cyclical setback. In *this* context, the argument in support of indexation deserves more careful analysis. Yet I believe (1) that at the stage of the process at which the United States finds itself now the indexation argument is nevertheless outright misleading and (2) that on assumptions which would be "ideal" for its validity the argument cannot be brushed aside but is quite a bit weaker than most of its proponents would lead one to think.

I will not distinguish a third category of inflationary processes—so-called commodity inflations—which are supposedly explained by a rise in specific prices in relation to others. According to the popular discussion that has developed mainly since 1973, food and energy prices are cases in point. Yet a steepened increase in specific prices does not itself explain why demand-management policies fail to use sufficient restraint to achieve a correspondingly lesser rate of increase in the other components of the GNP deflator.

Actual and Expected Inflation

From informal exchanges of views I have concluded that a meeting of minds on the indexation problem—at least a meeting of minds on the nature of the differences—is made easier by using terminology that fits into a simple and by now more or less conventional model. For most purposes this simple model has all along seemed too "aggregative" to me. But it is easy to make adjustments for its shortcomings and to grasp its implications.

In the terminology I shall be using, a state described by the proposition that "the expected rate of inflation" falls short of the actual rate of inflation should be visualized as a state in which policies are adopted that lead to more inflation than was expected by private decision makers when they entered contracts involving payment obligations for the period. The contrary is true of a state described by the proposition that "the expected rate of inflation" exceeds the actual rate.

We may regard the state in which the expected rate falls short of the actual as one in which (1) the typical wage earner underestimates the future rise of the consumer price index (CPI) and (2) the typical employer underestimates the prices that will be charged by those from whom he buys, that is, he overestimates his own future *relative prices.* When actual inflation is thus kept running ahead of inflationary expectations and a very large part of the public has in each phase entered into obligations expecting more real income than will prove to be available, comprehensive indexation of deferred payments would increase the difficulties that need to be faced. The authorities would have two options: (1) they could accommodate a further acceleration of the actual rate and also of the lagging expected rate of inflation, or (2) they could rely on monetary and fiscal restraint in an effort to reduce the actual rate to or below the current expected rate. But if they chose the second of these two options, they would probably have to carry out their policy of restraint in even more cumbersome circumstances than those in which such a policy would have to be put into effect in the absence of indexation.

Our Recent Inflation

I believe that in the United States we have been living for some time in an environment that can be described by an excess of the actual over the expected inflation rate in the sense here explained. Real wage and profit trends strongly suggest that inflation has been kept steep enough to disappoint most decision makers, ex post facto, concerning the real incomes they will be earning at the levels of activities which were being maintained. This is another way of saying that, in successive phases, obligations were entered into which implied the availability of a larger total real income than has in fact accrued to the typical parties accepting the obligations. In these circumstances the excess of actual over expected inflation keeps steepening the inflationary expectations. As a result, the whole process shows a pronounced tendency to accelerate.

In any country in which this kind of discrepancy between the actual and the expected rate continued to be generated, comprehensive indexation would lead to additional acceleration. Under indexation, money wages and other costs would be adjusted upward more rapidly because the fact that price inflation was proceeding more rapidly than had been expected would have a prompter effect on costs and hence also a prompter feedback on prices. Moreover, in the individual sectors decision makers expecting a faster rate of increase in the price measure used for indexation will probably *try* to move their prices even faster than the rate at which they expect the index to rise. The reason for this is that the hitherto existing relation between the typical seller's own prices, on the one hand, and the wage rates and the prices he *pays*, on the other, has been disappointing to him. Not being satisfied with his relative prices, he will try to raise them. Such a self-defeating inflationary process can be "beaten down" by monetary-fiscal restraint. However, comprehensive indexation would be apt to increase the resistance of the price trend to such restraint, and hence to increase the underutilization and the resulting hardships of the required adjustment period. This is so because of the existence of an initial tendency toward steepened inflation.

Assumptions More Favorable to the Indexation Argument

By pointing out that indexing would have harmful consequences in the type of disequilibrium we were considering, we have admittedly not met the issue of comprehensive indexation in general. What if the actual rate of inflation has already been reduced to the expected rate and the problem is that of stabilizing this lower rate? In response to this question, it may be suggested that if the authorities should be successful in establishing such an inflationary equilibrium, the markets would make allowances for the roughly predictable rate of general price increase without formal indexation. On the other hand, it may be argued that formal indexation of payment obligations, *even with reliance on some inevitably deficient index*, would have advantages as well as disadvantages in this case. However, the question of "promoting indexation" would be reduced to minor importance because of the allowances which the markets would make anyway for the roughly foreseen inflation rate.

But what if we are already in a condition in which the actual rate of inflation just about equals the initially given expected rate and we then seek a transition to a condition in which the actual rate will equal a *lowered* expected rate—say, a zero rate or at least a significantly reduced one? I think most proponents of comprehensive indexation have *this* problem in mind, or problems which in simplified terminology can be similarly described.

For example, assume that at the present writing we conclude from wage trends, interest rates, and other variables that "the expected rate of inflation" in the United States is somewhere around 7 percent a year, and assume further that we have reduced the actual rate to this number but want to reduce it to 3 percent or less, possibly to zero. Comprehensive indexation would then have the result that when general price increases successively decelerated to 5 percent, 4 percent, and so forth, the money wage rates earlier agreed upon would automatically follow suit. This is at least a potential advantage because it may promote further relatively painless price deceleration at the right time. But even when the argument becomes narrowed to the situation we are now considering, qualifications need to be added. It is easy to overestimate the strength of the argument because potential disadvantages must be set against the potential advantage rightly claimed.

I will limit myself here to calling attention to a complication developing from an inevitable time lag, one that makes it very likely that a reduction of a high equilibrium rate of inflation to a low one would be accompanied by a cyclical setback with or without indexation. Even with comprehensive indexing, individual decision makers must be willing to sell their goods at decelerating prices *before* indexing has led to a deceleration of their wage and other costs and without knowing *when* (or even *whether*) the cost deceleration will take place—because that deceleration, after all, depends on how other sellers of goods will behave and thus on how the price index will move. Only in an environment having the output and employment characteristics of a cyclical setback will price deceleration take place, *whether there is indexation or not.*

Furthermore, not only is it true that even under indexation the weakness of markets must force price deceleration prior to any wage deceleration brought about by indexing—the indexing of wages being presumably based on the CPI—but empirically it is also true that the timing of the CPI's deceleration relative to any individual seller's sale-and-price decision is quite uncertain. The proponents of indexing argue that under indexing wage deceleration follows an assumed price deceleration "automatically." The argument is valid but, as we shall see in a moment, no individual seller and no policy maker can make a reasonably dependable guess as to when the CPI would decelerate as a result of a policy of general monetary restraint. The individual seller knows only that this does not depend on his own sale-and-price decisions.

Factual statements on when price deceleration has started in some period are not clear-cut unless the spans over which prices are averaged as well as the spans over which price changes are measured are clearly stated, and it is uncertain how the technique of comprehensive indexation would be applied in these respects. Nevertheless, on the basis of the available data, it seems safe to suggest that the CPI decelerated during the recession of 1953-54, but did not decelerate at all *during* the recession of 1957-58 or *during* that of 1960-61. It is doubtful whether, even when we consider the special problem of reducing a higher equilibrium rate of inflation to a lower equilibrium rate, mechanical reliance on inevitably deficient index numbers is to be recommended, since the initial response of the price index to demand restraints and hence the induced wage response may well be forthcoming after a recession that has run its full course. This is illustrated by the recessions of 1957-58 and 1960-61 but not by that of 1969-70, *during* which the CPI did indeed start decelerating. There *is* a presumption that in the recession of 1969-70, as well as in that of 1953-54, indexing would have made the feedback of initially price-induced wage deceleration on prices more pronounced. Yet, taking the case of the recession of 1969-70, it is hard to imagine that wage agreements based on indexation would not have caused substantial difficulties of a different kind because it is hard to conceive of wage agreements stipulating so low a rise in *real* wage rates as the one which took place in that recession period.

Conclusions, Positive and Negative

While my appraisal of indexing has not turned me into a "fan," I am not as unbending in my negativism as some of the proponents are in their advocacy. As the reader has seen, I am aware of pros as well as cons when the problem is defined as that of reducing the actual rate of inflation from some currently expected rate to a lower expected *and* actual level. Also, I recognize that some of the allowances which markets would make for general price increases in any future, more or less stabilized "inflationary equilibrium" could be considered the equivalents of indexing. Indeed, in such a situation formula indexation itself might prove the smoothest method of incorporating the allowances into contracts *of some types*, despite the obvious inadequacies of all the available indices. However, I am firmly convinced that where we are faced with the consequences of the actual inflation rate having been kept above the expected rate. and with the resulting tendency of inflation to accelerate, comprehensive indexing would create significant additional difficulties. It would do so *both* on the pessimistic assumption that the same policy attitudes continue *and* on the more hopeful assumption that policy makers are at long last determined to put an end to a state of disequilibrium in which inflation is accelerating.

Even at the cost of a cyclical setback, policy makers must show this determination unless they are willing to stage a transition into a much more regimented economic and political system in which merely the symptoms of inflation would be suppressed. If they wake up to this danger, they will stop using their monetary and fiscal tools to generate increasingly steep inflation. Instead, they will use these tools with sufficient restraint so as to create an environment in which, after an unavoidable period of adjustment, the bulk of the private decision makers *becomes and remains aware of the risks of entering into obligations on terms and on a scale implying the unrealistic real-income expectations that develop under a lax policy.* To predict that such a change of policy attitudes would miscarry because the adjustment period would last too long and would be intolerably harsh means giving up on our society at a stage of its development where playing it always safe in one direction has proved an unsuccessful political strategy but the society itself has shown a great deal of staying power and vitality.

I should add two remarks. The first is that I do not extend my skepticism about indexing proposals to matters of taxation—that is, to the question of periodic adjustments of exemption limits, of deductions, of tax brackets, and to the determination of amounts on which capital gains taxes are levied. These matters involve political rather than market decisions, and it is clear that in a world where the general price level is rising, earlier decisions on tax provisions lead to unintended results. My second and final remark is that I have not tried to analyze a situation in which a significant reduction in a steep inflation rate is carried out with what essentially is effective regulation of wage rates, combined with restrained demand-management policies and supplemented by indexation. This is not the context relevant to the present American indexation debate, although adequate comparative analysis of specific problems arising in alternative political environments is, of course, of substantial interest.

4

INDEXING MONEY PAYMENTS IN A LARGE AND PROLONGED INFLATION

Edward M. Bernstein

The Rise of Prices, 1965-74

Since 1965, U.S. prices have risen almost without interruption. The wholesale price index of all commodities (1967=100) moved from 95.5 in March 1965 to 154.5 in March 1974, while the consumer price index of all items went up from 93.7 to 143.1 in the same period. This is the longest sustained rise of prices since the end of World War II. What is more, the rate of increase has accelerated in the past two years. In the twelve months to March 1973, the wholesale price index rose by 10.5 percent and the consumer price index by 4.7 percent. In the twelve months to March 1974, the wholesale price index rose by 19.1 percent and the consumer price index by 10.2 percent. Although special factors contributed to the very large increases for these two periods, the underlying inflationary pressures also increased.

This large and prolonged inflation has caused economic and social disruption. The uneven incidence of rapid price increases bears unfairly on the sectors of the community whose incomes cannot be promptly adjusted. The changes in the real value of capital assets make it difficult to protect the savings of the past or to safeguard savings for the future. The measures that people take to escape the windfall losses and to capture windfall gains involve a cost with no benefit to the economy. Governmental attempts to restrain the rise in prices and costs through controls distort the pattern of production. Perhaps worst of all, persistent inflation undermines public confidence in the capacity of the government to deal with economic problems.

Economists have long been aware of the disturbing effects of large price fluctuations. Under the gold standard, there was no way of avoiding the long waves of alternately rising and falling prices which were primarily due to excessive or inadequate gold production. It is interesting to note that, before the turn of the century, a number of economists were suggesting that the effects of price fluctuations could be minimized if money payments were linked to an index number—what they called a tabular standard. In 1887, in a memorandum to the Royal Commission on the Values of Gold and Silver, Alfred Marshall wrote:

> [The] time has arrived for inquiring whether we cannot adopt the suggestion made early in this century, that Government should publish a tabular standard of value for optional use within the United Kingdom in all transactions which extend over a long period of time. It could be used, for instance, in long leases, in mortgages, and all other borrowings of capital for long periods, and even in such contracts formal or informal for the hire of labour and personal services as are of long duration. A theoretically perfect standard of purchasing power is unattainable; and it would probably be best, for the sake of simplicity, to begin with a comparatively rough standard. But the index-numbers with which we are already familiar would give a ten times better standard of value for optional use within the country in long-standing contracts than even a true bimetallic currency [one combining both gold and silver].

The present inflation has not been imposed on the world by unavoidable circumstances. It is the consequence of the financial policies of governments. Despite good intentions, governments have been completely unsuccessful in their attempts to slow and to halt the inflation. This is the reason for the recent flood of proposals for a formal link between wages, long-term loans, and some other monetary payments on the one hand and an index of prices on the other. Strangely, a few economists favor such a plan because they believe that the greatest harm done by inflation is not the shift of real income or the distortion of production, but rather the unemployment resulting from tight monetary and budget policies designed to halt the inflation. Some regard the indexing of money payments as a way of insulating the real incomes of some sectors from the inequitable effects of inflation. Still others believe that an indexing system would make it more possible for anti-inflationary measures to succeed. On the other hand, there are economists who oppose indexing on the grounds that it would increase the difficulty of restoring monetary stability.

Indexing Wages

In any prolonged inflation, wage increases will be more or less affected by the rise in consumer prices and by expectations of a further rise in prices. The practical question, therefore, is what would be gained by establishing a formal link, perhaps by legislation, between wage increases and the rise in prices. The most obvious answer is that this would be fair to workers, particularly those who are not in a strong bargaining position. The Bureau of Labor Statistics reports that the real disposable income of wage earners, after adjusting the increase in money earnings for the rise in consumer prices and higher tax payments, fell by 4.7 percent in the twelve months to March 1974. This is an example of why some economists regard it as necessary to index wages in the interest of providing justice for workers.

The view that indexing is necessary to protect the real income of wage earners in a prolonged inflation is based on a number of implicit assumptions. The first is that inflation shifts a larger share of output to profits and that this shift should be corrected by an increase in wages. The second is that the rise in the consumer price index measures this shift. The third is that the increase in wages to offset the rise in the consumer price index will succeed in increasing real wages to the same extent—that is, that it will not be offset in whole or in large part by a further rise of prices. Finally, it is assumed that if labor were assured of wage adjustments linked to the rise in the consumer price index, demands for basic wage increases would become more moderate, thus making it possible to slow the inflation gradually, and eventually to stop it. Most, if not all, of these assumptions are unjustified, certainly under present conditions.

Proposals to link the increase of wages to the rise of prices raise a number of technical problems. One is that the consumer price index has an upward trend even when wholesale prices of manufactured goods are stable. Thus, in the five years between 1959 and 1964, prices of manufactured goods rose by 0.2 percent, while consumer prices rose by 6.4 percent. This divergence between these two price indexes is typical for a period of monetary stability. Allowance can be made in any system of indexing for the trend rise in the consumer price index, which averages about 1.2 percent a year in periods of monetary stability. Even in inflation, however, there are occasions when the rise in consumer prices is very large for reasons that would not require, on economic grounds, an offsetting increase in wages. Under such conditions, if wage increases were linked to the rise in the consumer price index, it could only result in accelerated inflation. This can be illustrated by recent price developments.

In the twelve months to March 1974, the consumer price index rose by 10.2 percent. Prices of food, with a relative importance of 24.8 percent in the total index, rose by 18.3 percent and accounted for slightly less than half of the entire rise in the consumer price index. The rise in food prices was caused by a number of unusual conditions. According to *Survey of Current Business* (April 1974), gross farm product in 1958 dollars fell from an annual rate of $24.8 billion in the first quarter of 1973 to $23.2 billion in the first quarter of 1974. This 6.5 percent decline in gross farm product came at a time when there was an even larger shortfall in farm production abroad and an enormous increase in U.S. exports of food and feedingstuffs. There is no way to insulate the real income of wage earners from the effects of a decline in farm production in this country and, except by restricting food exports, of crop failures abroad as well. An increase in wages to offset the rise in food prices would only lead to still higher prices of food, with very little increase in the amount available for consumption. It would also lead to a rise in the prices of other goods and services because production costs would be increased as a result of the adjustment of wages in response to the rise in the consumer price index.

Another factor in the recent large rise in the consumer price index was the sharp increase in fuel prices. In the twelve months to March 1974, prices for gasoline and motor oil rose by 39.3 percent and prices for fuel oil and coal by 57.7 percent. Although these commodities have a relative importance of only 4.0 percent in the consumer price index, the rise in their prices accounted for over 17 percent of the rise in the entire index. Much of the rise in prices for oil and oil products went as payments to the oil-exporting countries. There is no way in which the higher cost of imported oil can be offset by transferring income from other sectors to workers through an increase of wages. That would not bring down the price of oil, although it could lead to more imports, and it would result in a further rise in the prices of other goods and services. To put it simply, there is no way to insulate wage earners from an adverse change in the terms of trade.

The same analysis applies more generally to the price effects of the dollar's devaluation in February 1973 and its subsequent de facto depreciation relative to the currencies in the European common float. The unit value of U.S. imports, a rough index of import prices, rose by 47.5 percent between March 1973 and March 1974. Not all of the rise can be attributed to the depreciation of the dollar, because the rest of the world was inflating about as much as the United States.

Perhaps more important for the consumer price index, part of the increase in the prices of basic commodities, those exported as well as those imported, was directly due to the depreciation of the dollar. If a rise in the consumer price index resulting from a change in the foreign exchange value of the dollar must be offset by an increase in wages, the beneficial effect of the depreciation of the dollar on the balance of payments would be largely negated. The inevitable consequence would be a cumulative depreciation of the dollar and an accelerated inflation.

It can be argued that these are special cases and that an indexing system could take them into account. Even then, there would still be the objection that not every rise in prices justifies an offsetting increase in wages. The effect of farm products and imported goods on prices can be eliminated by using the implicit price deflator of the gross product originating in nonfinancial corporations. This is probably the best measure of the impact of domestic demand and cost inflation on prices. Between the fourth quarter of 1972 and the fourth quarter of 1973, the consumer price index rose by 8.4 percent while the implicit price deflator of the gross product of nonfinancial corporations rose by 4.6 percent. Of this rise, 85 percent was caused by the increase in labor compensation per unit of output, nearly 7 percent by the increase in capital consumption allowances, nearly 2 percent by indirect business taxes, and nearly 7 percent by the increase in corporate profits and inventory valuation adjustment. In these four quarters, the share of labor compensation in the gross product of nonfinancial corporations increased from 66.0 to 66.8 percent and the share of profits and inventory valuation adjustment was reduced from 11.5 to 11.2 percent.

Suppose that wages had to be adjusted to offset the increase in the implicit price deflator—in addition, of course, to the increase in wages corresponding to the trend increase in productivity. The wage adjustment could not come from capital consumption allowances, indirect business taxes, or interest. Very little of it could come from profits, as their share in output has declined considerably in recent years. As a practical matter, the increase in wages would have to be accompanied by an almost equivalent increase in prices. Simple logic would indicate that if a rise in the implicit price deflator that was almost entirely due to an increase in unit labor cost had to be offset by a further increase in wages, there would be no way to avoid a rapidly ascending price-wage spiral. The ultimate in nonsense economics would be reached if a decline in productivity (output per manhour) were to become the justification for an increase in wages because it had caused a rise in unit labor cost and in the implicit price deflator.

One further point can be made regarding the consumer price index. The prices in this index are retail prices including tax. A small part of the rise in the consumer price index in recent years is attributable to the increase in sales taxes by states and municipalities, although there has also been a reduction in some federal excise taxes. If wages are to be adjusted for a rise in the consumer price index, including that part of it caused by higher taxes, wage earners would in effect be exempt from any increase in sales and excise taxes. These taxes may not be ideal for raising revenues, but that is not a good reason why wages and salaries, which comprise two-thirds of total personal income, should be protected against increases in sales and excise taxes.

In general, labor is entitled to a wage adjustment when the consumer price index rises by more than the 1.2 percent a year average under conditions of monetary stability. If wages are at a level consistent with the maintenance of stability—that is, the trend share of labor compensation in output—the adjustment could be about equal to the increase in consumer prices in excess of 1.2 percent a year. That is typically the case in a demand inflation, when the share of labor compensation falls and the share of profits rise, as it did in the United States in 1965-66. Under such conditions it may be assumed that, if excess demand is eliminated, most of the increase in wages would be absorbed in a decrease in the share of profits. Even then, the precise amount of the adjustment that is justified cannot be measured by the rise in the consumer price index. It depends very much on the specific causes of the rise in prices.

Since 1967 the United States has had a cost inflation in which the share of labor compensation in output has risen considerably above the trend of the past two decades. Under such conditions, it is not possible to give an offsetting increase in wages to match the rise in consumer prices without accelerating the inflation. Provision for an appropriate adjustment can be better made through collective bargaining agreements which avoid a rigid link between the increase in wages and the rise in consumer prices. That is done by providing for a threshold before a rise in prices necessitates an increase in wages, by limiting the adjustment to a proportion of the rise in prices, and by placing a ceiling on the wage adjustment. Moreover, collective bargaining agreements usually take account of the special factors that affect an industry. To put it simply, collective bargaining can make ample allowance for adjusting wages in a period of inflation with greater flexibility than could be achieved by a government requirement for indexing.

Indexing Payments on Loans

Proposals for linking payments on long-term loans to the rise of prices antedate those for indexing wages. There are a number of reasons for this. Wage agreements are usually for relatively short periods. A large proportion of the labor force is employed either without formal agreements or under one-year agreements. Even major collective bargaining agreements are almost never for periods longer than three years. Thus, post-agreement adjustments in wages can be made to take account of a larger than expected rise in the consumer price index before real wages have been seriously impaired. Besides, some agreements already make provision for an adjustment of wages after a threshold rise in the consumer price index. Finally, even major collective bargaining agreements can be reopened for renegotiation of wages if they become manifestly unfair.

The situation is quite different for loans which are made for long periods. Lenders and borrowers have no means of changing the original terms of the loan, regardless of the behavior of prices and interest rates. Some bonds may have a call feature for redemption before maturity that protects the borrower, not the lender, from the risk of a future fall in interest rates. Other bonds may have a sinking fund feature under which a part of the issue is retired annually, but if the bonds are drawn by lot this gives the lender very little protection against an unexpected rise in prices and interest rates. Loan agreements are binding for the full period of the loan. Except in the event of bankruptcy, the terms of the loan cannot be renegotiated. For these reasons, lenders are fully exposed to the risks of an unexpected rise in prices and interest rates. Their only practical means of protection is to shorten the maturities of their loans, so that a new interest rate is determined at relatively frequent intervals. That would allow for the direct and indirect effects of inflation on interest rates.

The inflation risk could be reduced to a considerable extent by linking the payment of interest and the repayment of principal of a loan at maturity to the change in an agreed index of prices—the reference index. Thus, the loan would provide a basic interest rate— say, 4 percent per annum. At each interest payment date, the amount of interest payable would be adjusted for the rise or fall in the reference index since the loan was made. If the reference index were 5 percent higher at the end of the first year, 10 percent higher at the end of the second year, and 15 percent higher at the end of the third year, the actual interest payments would be 4.2 percent of the nominal principal at the end of the first year, 4.4 percent at the end of the second year, and 4.6 percent at the end of the third year. At maturity, the principal to be repaid would be the nominal amount of the loan adjusted for the change in the reference index. If that price index rose by 100 percent in the course of a twenty-year loan, the principal due at maturity would be double the amount of the loan.

Most of the objections to the indexing of wages also apply to the indexing of long-term loans. In the case of wages, the most appropriate index would seem to be that of consumer prices, although provision could be made in various ways for adjustment when extraordinary factors caused a large rise in the index. Long-term loans could be linked to another index more representative of the rise in business prices or costs during an inflation. Thus, the reference index could be the wholesale price index of manufactured goods or the implicit price deflator of the gross product originating in nonfinancial corporations. The choice of a reference index would not be of great significance, because allowance could be made for the usual differences in the typical behavior of the alternative indexes, and because the relative rise in the different indexes would probably not diverge much in a period of ten or twenty years from what had been expected.

The practical problems would be more important. Presumably, indexing would be confined to medium-term and long-term loans, as it would not be possible to index short-term loans, including savings deposits, three-month Treasury bills, and business loans. Thus, financial institutions, which are both lenders and borrowers, would have most of their liabilities in fixed-dollar obligations, whereas some of their assets, those indexed, would have a variable-dollar value. This might not present difficulties for life insurance companies since they could write policies linked to the money value of the reserves they hold against such policies. Deposit institutions, such as banks and savings and loan associations, would have greater difficulty in managing their assets and liabilities. Presumably, they would have the option of making unindexed loans, and they would undoubtedly find borrowers that preferred to have the interest and principal of the loan expressed in a fixed-money amount.

It is implicitly assumed by those favoring the indexing of long-term loans that the real interest rate should be the same under inflation as under conditions of monetary stability. That is not necessarily so. The interest rate that borrowers would be prepared to pay depends on the type of inflation and that cannot be determined with reference to an index of prices. Thus, the implicit price deflator of the product of nonfinancial corporations could rise by 5 percent as the result of a large increase in unit costs for labor and other factors, with little or no increase in profits per unit of output. Or the implicit price deflator could rise by 5 percent with a moderate increase in unit costs for labor and other factors and a considerable increase in profits per unit of output. In the latter case (demand inflation), interest rates could even rise more than prices. In the former case (cost inflation), interest rates would probably not rise as much as prices. This was recognized by Knut Wicksell in his *Interest and Prices,* in which he said:

> According to my view, a rise in prices . . . is usually due to a rise in the entrepreneurs' demand for labour and other productive services. Such a rise in prices is thus the consequence of a previous, no matter how far from uniform, rise in money wages and rents, and it merely serves to compensate the entrepreneurs for the rise in costs of production. It does not provide them with the means of paying a higher rate of interest.

So the basic question is whether the indexing of loans is necessary in order to take account of inflation. The money and capital markets determine interest rates on the basis of the supply of and demand for loanable funds. These interest rates include a premium for inflation. They are, however, determined by market forces that take other factors into account besides inflation. There is nothing to prevent any lender from treating part of the interest payment as amortization of the real value of the capital, which is what the inflation premium really is. The greater variability of interest rates under inflationary conditions does create a problem for institutions that make medium-term and long-term loans at fixed interest rates while the interest rates they pay on deposits vary with market conditions. In practice banks overcome this difficulty by linking the interest rate on their medium-term loans to the prime rate on short-term business loans which is related to the rate they pay on large denomination certificates of deposit. In the Eurocurrency market, the rate on medium-term loans is linked to the interbank rate on deposits. Savings and loan associations have a more serious problem. Their problem could be solved by linking the mortgage rates they charge to the rates they pay on savings. That would seem to be simpler and better than linking mortgage loans to an index of prices.

The purpose of indexing loans must be concern over the effect of inflation on personal savings and on small savers. In fact, the personal saving rate has been higher during the inflation than it was before. In part this may be due to the need to restore the real value of cash balances and of savings held in money assets as prices rise. The very large increase in food prices that impaired the real income of wage earners in 1973 did hold down the personal savings rate, except in the fourth quarter when the oil shortage resulted in a large fall in consumer expenditures on automobiles and parts. But there are still no signs that personal savings are being discouraged by inflation. The deficiency in private saving has actually been in corporate saving, where retained earnings have been a declining proportion of the value of output after adjustment is made for taxes on fictitious inventory profits and for inadequate capital consumption allowances.

Much more important as a social problem is the considerable loss in the real value of accumulated personal savings held in monetary form. People of moderate means hold much of their savings in the form of deposits, and such people have been very inadequately compensated for the inflation because interest rates on such savings have risen much less than money market rates. That is partly due to the continuation of ceilings on time and savings deposits, although since November 1973 savings institutions have been permitted to pay 7¼ percent on savings certificates in minimum denominations of $1,000 issued for a period of four years or longer. The interest rate on U.S. government savings bonds held to maturity is 6 percent, which is too far below market rates. There is great justification for providing small savers with a better real return. But this could be done much better through higher interest rates on small savings than through indexing, particularly since there is no convenient way of linking savings deposits to the rise in prices.

Indexing Federal Taxes

Large and persistent budget deficits are a major cause of inflation. In the past, it was frequently argued that the inflation itself caused budget deficits to increase and that this was one way in which the inflation became self-generating. That was probably true in countries with rapid inflation, because governments had to respond rather quickly in the prices and salaries they paid, while collection of taxes on income and profits was long delayed—as much as five or six quarters after the beginning of the year in which they were earned. It is not true, however, in countries where inflation is more moderate and where taxes are paid on income and profits as they are earned or very soon thereafter.

In the United States, the effect of the inflation has been to hold down the budget deficit. Payments for supplies increase with the rise in prices, but the adjustment of salaries is delayed. For example, higher civil servants have received no salary increases at all in the past five years. About the only budget payment that has increased much more than prices, and has also risen considerably relative to the gross national product, is interest on the public debt. Between fiscal 1965 and fiscal 1974, interest payments increased from $10.4 billion to about $27.8 billion. Nearly half of the increase is attributable to higher interest rates. The average rate on the total interest-bearing public debt rose from 3.7 percent in June 1965 to about 6.5 percent in May 1974—proportionately much more than any broad price index over that period. It should be noted, however, that most of the increase in the interest rate represents amortization of the real value of the debt. In fact, despite the enormous deficits during that period, the ratio of federal debt to gross national product declined from 49.9 percent in June 1965 to about 36.3 percent in the second quarter of 1974.

Tax revenues are very favorably affected by inflation. That is because the tax system has a built-in bias toward higher taxes when prices and incomes rise. In the United States, the personal exemption in the income tax remained unchanged at $600 per taxpayer and dependent from 1948 to 1969, and then was raised in $50 yearly increments to $750 in 1972. Moreover, the tax brackets have not been changed since 1964. As a consequence and given the cumulative rise in money wages, low real incomes that were untaxed prior to the inflation have become taxable, and real incomes that were taxed at the basic rate before the inflation have become subject to the higher graduated rates. This bias in the income tax structure is of small importance to persons in the higher brackets. It is a serious burden to wage earners, however, because their real disposable income is held down by the resulting excessive increases in their taxes.

A very strong case can be made in favor of increasing income taxes in a period of inflation. The objection is not to the increase in taxes, but to the arbitrary incidence of the increase among different taxpayers and on different forms of income. If the United States is to tolerate prolonged inflation, it should, in equity, change the basis for levying personal income taxes. One change would be to link the amount of the personal exemption to the consumer price index. It may not be economically desirable always to increase wages to the same extent as the rise in consumer prices; it is socially necessary to raise the personal exemption to the full extent of the increase in the cost of living. Much the same argument applies to the linking of the graduated income tax brackets, at least the lower ones, to the rise in the consumer price index. It should be noted that social security tax legislation already links the wage base for the payroll tax to the index of consumer prices.

The inequity produced by the personal income tax during periods of inflation is even more marked in the taxation of interest income. Nearly all of the increase in the interest rate attributable to inflation is actually an amortization payment on real capital. Thus, if the interest rate rises from 4 to 8 percent because of inflation, a taxpayer with a marginal rate of 50 percent would in effect be paying an annual tax of about 2 percent on the nominal value of his principal. Over the life of a twenfy-year bond, the government would have imposed a capital levy of one-third on the original real value of the principal. It is true that this hardship on persons receiving interest income could be avoided by indexing the principal of bonds, provided the government did not treat as income the sum paid at maturity that would be in excess of the original amount of the loan. Even if treated as a capital gain, however, the tax would be a levy, although a smaller one, on the real value of the capital of the lender.

The taxation of corporate profits also involves a capital levy in the guise of an income tax. True profits, even in money terms, represent what a corporation earns after making provision to keep its real capital intact. In the national accounts, this is shown as profits and inventory valuation adjustment—that is, adjustment for replacing at current cost the raw materials and components used in production. The tax law, however, treats the difference between the original cost of inventories and their replacement cost as taxable profits. In 1973, when the real output of nonfinancial corporations increased by 7.8 percent, profits and inventory valuation adjustment increased from $69.3 billion to $78.2 billion. Because of the accelerated inflation, the notional profits resulting from the use of earlier stocks in production increased from $7.0 billion to $17.6 billion. After corporations paid taxes on their true and notional profits and restored their original inventories, they had available for dividends and retained earnings $37.4 billion in 1973 compared with $36.0 billion in 1972. As a share of the gross product originating in nonfinancial corporations, profits after tax and inventory valuation adjustment fell from 5.9 percent to 5.5 percent. This decline in true after-tax profits per dollar of output was entirely due to the capital levy on the fictitious inventory profits resulting from inflation.

Much the same is true of capital consumption allowances. In 1973, the capital consumption allowances of nonfinancial corporations amounted to $68.1 billion. These allowances were based on the original cost of the plant and equipment used in production. However, if they had been based on replacement cost, which is the proper way to calculate true profits, they would have been about $4.3 billion higher on a straight line basis and about $11.0 billion higher on a double declining balance basis. In effect, corporate profits were overstated to this extent. The tax on such fictitious profits was a capital levy on the plant and equipment used in production.

If corporations were allowed to keep their accounts to reflect the results of their operations, undistorted by inflation, the profits they would report in current dollars would be profits after restoring their inventories and after depreciating their plant and equipment at replacement cost. There is no need for formal indexing to achieve this purpose. Corporations are well aware of the replacement cost of the inventories and the plant and equipment they use in production. What is needed is a recognition in the tax system that the present method of computing taxable profits includes notional profits that actually represent a reduction in the real capital of the corporation.

These inequities in the personal income and corporate profits tax are the result of inflation. An adjustment of the tax structure to avoid inflation distortions would result in a reduction in tax revenues. If this were done without a simultaneous adjustment of tax rates, it would increase the budget deficit and add to the inflationary pressures. That is not an argument against making the necessary adjustments now, particularly for personal exemptions and the lower tax brackets. It is rather a plea for coupling such adjustments with an increase in tax rates on higher incomes.

Will Indexing Slow the Inflation?

The general conclusion is that there is no need in the United States for formal indexing of wages and long-term loans on the grounds of equity. In the case of long-term loans, the market already makes the necessary adjustment through higher interest rates reflecting expectations on inflation. In the case of wages, collective bargaining agreements already take account of past inflation and expectations of further inflation, in some instances by linking price increases to wage increases. These adjustments to inflation are made more flexibly, and with fuller consideration of other factors, than would be possible in formal indexing under government sponsorship. Much of the hardship that inflation imposes on small savers and low-income taxpayers is the consequence of government regulations and could be remedied by the government. Pensions and social security payments are the only form of income for which indexing is fully justified, without regard to the cause of the rise in consumer prices. That justification is not so much a matter of equity as of need.

If indexing of wages and other money payments is desirable, it must be because it is believed that it will help to slow the inflation. There are countries in which very rapid inflation is accompanied by massive wage increases. In such cases the inflation is inherently accelerating. Where these circumstances exist it may be helpful to link wage increases to the rise in consumer prices, although with safeguards of various kinds, in order to hold down massive wage increases. The United States is not confronted with this problem. At best, the indexing of wages in the United States would institutionalize and stabilize the rate of inflation. If the consumer price index were to rise by 6 percent, and if 6 percent had to be added to the basic increase in wages—the productivity component—then unit labor cost would increase to about this extent and the consumer price index would again rise by 6 percent or more, unless favorable factors held down the rise of some prices. It should be apparent that if wages in the United States had been linked to the consumer price index in 1973, and if there had been no allowance for unusual conditions, the 1973 inflation rate would have been built into the economy for several years to come.

The case for indexing as a means of slowing inflation has been supported more by the example of Brazil than by an analysis of how it could be applied in the United States. The rise in the consumer price index in Brazil has been reduced from 87 percent in 1964 to about 15 percent in 1973. This is a remarkable achievement, even though the index is heavily weighted with official or controlled prices. If indexing has been the major factor in slowing the inflation in Brazil, it is because it is accompanied by rigid control over the increase in basic wages. In fact, that can be the only purpose of indexing— to justify control of the increase in basic wages. Such a policy would not be possible in the United States in the absence of price controls. With due regard for the emphasis placed on indexing in the case of Brazil, it is probable that the reduction of the budget deficit from 28 percent of expenditures in 1964 to a modest surplus in 1973 was of greater importance in slowing inflation.

There is no painless or costless way of slowing and halting inflation. An inflation can be ended only through fiscal and monetary policies persistently maintained to hold down the pressure of excessive expenditure. The United States has not had such policies. The unified budget has been in continuous deficit since fiscal year 1958, except for a surplus of $3.2 billion in 1969. In the three fiscal years 1971-73, the cumulative deficit was $60.6 billion. For the two years 1974-75, the deficit is estimated at $14 billion. Tolerance of continued large deficits has been rationalized on the grounds that the budget would be in balance with full employment. This ignores the fact that full employment as defined for budget purposes—an unemployment rate of 4 percent—is no longer attainable without chronic inflation.

Monetary policy has not been without fault either. Even when it has not been itself the initiating factor in inflation, it has been permissive—by providing an expansion of money and credit that supported a higher level of aggregate demand than the economy could supply without inflation. In the three years from December 1970 to December 1973, the money supply (currency plus demand deposits) increased at an average annual rate of 7.0 percent, the broader money supply (including time and savings deposits at commercial banks, but not large denomination certificates of deposit) increased at an average rate of 10.0 percent, and loans and investments of commercial banks increased at an average rate of 12.8 percent. This may not seem excessive from a liquidity point of view, given the fact that GNP increased in the three years at an average annual rate of 9.6 percent in current dollars and 5.2 percent in constant dollars. It was too easy a policy for a period of inflation, however, particularly after the devaluation of the dollar.

The United States is now at a critical point in dealing with inflation. On a national accounts basis, the budget deficit fell from $17.5 billion in calendar 1972 to $5.6 billion in calendar 1973, mainly because of the inflation-induced increase in tax revenues. The deficit (NIA basis) may fall further this year because of the continued inflation, despite the current decline in output and employment. This decline has again called forth in the Congress a spate of proposals to reduce taxes—that is, to increase the budget deficit. If every decline in employment is dealt with by reducing taxes, the United States will have perpetual inflation.

Monetary policy has been tightened somewhat since March 1974, and it is unlikely to be relaxed until there are clear signs that the inflation is being slowed. In a statement to the House Banking and Currency Committee on 4 April 1974, Dr. Arthur F. Burns, chairman of the Federal Reserve Board, said: "[We] at the Federal Reserve are determined to follow a course of monetary policy that will permit only moderate growth of money and credit. Such a policy should make it possible for the fires of inflation to burn themselves out, while it at the same time provides the financial basis for the resumption of orderly economic growth." To emphasize this policy, the Federal Reserve has now raised the discount rate to 8.0 percent.

Fiscal and monetary policies designed to slow the inflation will be helped by more favorable supply and price conditions. The special factors that have contributed so much to the accelerated rise in prices since February 1973 are about over, although they have not as yet been fully passed through in consumer prices. Output of farm products in the United States and other important food-exporting countries will increase this year. The price of oil will not be raised again, and it is possible that it may decline somewhat after a few months. The effect of the dollar's devaluation on the prices of import goods, particularly basic commodities, is about over. There is also the possibility that the dollar will become somewhat stronger in the exchange market. Not enough emphasis has been given to the large amount of domestic output that, until recently, had to be devoted to restoring the balance of payments and to compensating for the adverse change in the terms of trade. Between the fourth quarter of 1972 and the first quarter of 1974, the increase in U.S. exports of goods and services in constant 1958 dollars exceeded the increase of such imports by $13.4 billion a year. This absorbed over 80 percent of the increase in real output in this period. That drain on output will not recur until the higher cost of imported oil is paid for by increased exports.

If price and supply developments follow a favorable course, the cautious fiscal and monetary policies of the administration and the Federal Reserve will succeed in slowing the inflation, although that will take time. It is essential, however, not to give way to the pressure to ease these policies in order to stimulate a prompt and large recovery of output and employment. The key to dealing with an inflation that has become imbedded in the economy is to persist in the effort to eradicate it through fiscal and monetary policies. The indexing of money payments is irrelevant to the inflation problem in the United States.

5

INDEXING FOR INFLATION IN BRAZIL

Alexandre Kafka

This paper briefly (1) describes the Brazilian system of generalized indexing or escalator clauses, sometimes called "monetary correction," (2) examines the chief economic developments since the introduction of generalized indexing, and (3) draws some tentative conclusions about how the system works in Brazil and makes some even more tentative generalizations.

Description

Due to the extremely rapid inflation which had prevailed in Brazil beginning with the early fifties, some rent contracts and the progressive personal income tax schedule were indexed even before 1964, and indices played a role in wage determination. It was not until 1964, however, that indexing became generally used, although it is not universal.

Labor. Statutory minimum wages and government salaries had long been influenced by cost-of-living indices, as had wage negotiations and the binding awards of labor courts with respect to other wages. Beginning about 1954, however, many observers felt that the use of indices did not prevent wage adjustments that were frequently "too high," that is, exerted an inflationary pressure which was quickly and invariably accommodated by monetary expansion.

A new system of wage adjustment was established in 1964 and reformed in one fundamental respect in 1968. Under the new system, all collective wage negotiations and labor court awards are subjected to guidelines which are established each month by the government. All contracts or awards remain in force for twelve months. The guidelines are not simple price indices but rather correspond to a formula with three basic components: past real wages, prospective inflation and prospective productivity increases. Guidelines based only on the first two factors are used to determine annual adjustments in statutory minimum wages (which are regionally differentiated, but gradually being equalized) and government salaries.

The first component is an index designed to reestablish, on the day of adjustment, the average real wage which had prevailed over the preceding twenty-four months. The cost-of-living index is used in these calculations. It was assumed on the institution of the system that, over such a lengthy period, the rate of inflation and the money wage level (in the absence of observed guidelines) would have adjusted to each other and established that real wage level which was compatible with the extent of unemployment (and, more importantly, of underemployment) which the economy found tolerable. In other words, a money wage level set so as to produce the real wage level just described will be neither inflationary nor deflationary. A money wage adjusted to reproduce the real wage level at some specific past date, on the other hand, might be unrealistically high, leading to unemployment (or too low).

The second component is a term reflecting prospective inflation because it was realized that inflation would have to be allowed to continue for some time, irrespective of the wage policy followed. There were three principal reasons for this: (1) In order to dampen inflationary expectations, formerly repressed prices should not be adjusted to their equilibrium levels at once but gradually—that is, "corrective inflation" was to be gradual. (2) There was a huge budget deficit (equal to nearly 5 percent of GNP) which had initially to be financed mainly by borrowing from the monetary authorities. (3) Long-term contracts had been entered into in the expectation of very high rates of inflation, and sudden elimination of inflation would have produced not only a liquidity crisis but also a genuine stabilization crisis. Accordingly, because of the expectation of continued inflation, half of the prospective rate of inflation for the next twelve months was added to the money wage established in accordance with the basic formula. On the assumption of a linear monthly increase in prices, this is, of course, exactly the addition which would maintain average real wages constant over the twelve-month period.

Even after the principal controllable independent factors of inflation had been largely eliminated, some allowance for prospective inflation was maintained. This was done mainly to preserve government credibility in the event that price increases should result from either an unforeseeable or uncontrollable cause (like a bad harvest or a world price increase) or the pursuit of a credit policy designed, despite its gradual disinflationary stance, to avoid any liquidity crises.

In the first years of the new system, prospective inflation was repeatedly underestimated in setting guidelines, and real minimum wages—as well as average wages in some sectors—fell. Therefore, in 1968 the formula was revised in one fundamental respect. The money wage adjustment henceforth was based not on the actual average real wage of the preceding twenty-four months, but on what the real wage would have been if the prospective inflation had been correctly estimated at the time of the preceding adjustments.

The third component is a term reflecting the expected economy-wide increase in productivity per worker. Since Brazil was then (and even is today in some respects) a labor surplus economy, where the absorption of unemployment and underemployment requires emphasis, prospective productivity increases for incorporation into money wage adjustments must be conservatively estimated if, given the degree of price inflation to be tolerated, one is to avoid jeopardizing employment creation and thereby overall growth. It is with the same objective in mind that the adjustment of minimum wages, which for some years now has directly affected only unskilled labor in the less-developed regions of Brazil, takes no account of productivity increases.

The functional relationship between real wages, money wages and the rate of inflation makes it theoretically possible to produce the real wage level compatible with the desirable level of employment indifferently by adjustment of the money wage or by that of the rate of inflation. From the practical point of view, the incorporation into the wage formula of terms for prospective inflation, general productivity increases or the underestimation of prospective inflation in the setting of past guidelines has appeared more palatable all around. It is also clear that whatever the effect of these terms on the rate of inflation prevailing at any one time, their incorporation in the wage formula need not and did not by any means prevent a gradual reduction in the rate of inflation over the years.

Social security pensions, as well as government pensions, are also indexed according to the cost of living. Although the Brazilian social security system is based on the principle of full actuarial value, the federal government is residually responsible for any cash deficits. Actually, the growth of the system has prevented any cash problems from arising.

Capital. While the change in the system of wage determination made in 1964 was a profound one, the change in the remuneration of capital, which occurred subsequently, was even more radical. Inflation—combined with a usury law which set maximum interest rates of 12 percent—had made financial intermediation difficult. Various ways had been found to cope with these difficulties, but even the complete elimination of the usury law and the payment of high interest rates could not have solved the problems which high rates of inflation created for the capital market. Under such inflationary conditions, the possibility that the inflation rate will change is likely to lead to such uncertainty that, other things being equal, only very small sums will be borrowed or lent at any particular nominal interest rate. The solution to the problem is to reduce uncertainty to the unavoidable minimum, namely, to uncertainty only about changes in the real interest rate over the period of a credit or loan. This can be done by indexing, and this was the system gradually extended to different classes of credits or loans.

Credits or loans with variable interest rates would be an alternative method, if one could find a short-term interest rate which would be sure to reflect inflation correctly and to which the variable rate could be tied. Eurocurrency loan rates are tied to the London Interbank rate, and the variable interest rate on medium-term securities recently issued by some U.S. bank holding companies has been tied to the U.S. Treasury bill rate, but this does not mean that the two rates mentioned adequately reflect inflation. There was certainly no appropriate short-term interest rate in existence in Brazil in 1964 and money illusion is quite capable of preventing its appearance as long as the expected rate of inflation would imply a shockingly high level of the nominal interest rate compared to the traditional range of nominal interest rates. Even where there exists an appropriate short-term rate to which a variable rate for medium- or long-term securities or contracts can be tied, other considerations may recommend indexing over variable rates. There might be a desire clearly to distinguish between real interest and the effect of inflation, for political reasons as well as for reasons related to the tax system.

At first, indexing of credits and loans—based on the wholesale price index—was applied to Treasury bond issues that firms were obliged to purchase. Shortly afterwards, owners of these bonds were given the option of receiving payments on the basis of the exchange rate of the cruzeiro in terms of the U.S. dollar, rather than on the basis of the wholesale price index. With the change in the exchange system (to be discussed later), however, it turned out that in the presence of worldwide inflation, the Brazilian wholesale price index was a much better protector against inflation than the exchange rate.

The indexing feature on Treasury bonds means that, at regular intervals, an index number is published giving the corrected nominal value of the bond and the amount of interest payable is adjusted accordingly. At maturity the bond is redeemed in cash at its corrected value. Its sale and purchase before maturity and its acceptability as a guarantee (for example, where performance bonds are required) always takes into account the corrected value. Within a few years, the compulsory purchase of bonds had been abandoned and voluntary issues of indexed Treasury bonds had become acceptable. Most of these bonds have relatively short maturities, from one to two years, but some have maturities of up to five years (longer-term bonds have not been issued recently). They presently carry interest rates of between 4 and 6 percent.

Indexing on the same basis as on Treasury bonds was also applied to mortgage bills and contracts and has contributed greatly to the success of the housing finance system which was introduced after 1964.

Indexing is, of course, also available for other securities, including state government bonds, corporate bonds or debentures, bills, promissory notes, and loan contracts. The periodic writing up—that is, upward revaluation—of assets of corporations enables them to issue bonus shares. Corporate bond issues have been hampered because, for a variety of reasons which also affect equity issues, the market has not yet become accustomed to genuinely long-term bonds. In addition there is no incentive for industries to issue bonds rather than to obtain other financing, especially from official banks. (Official banks, in turn, finance themselves on term deposits as well as on budgetary contributions and loans raised abroad; they lend at long term and take equity participations.)

Subsequently, indexing was also applied to savings deposits and has more recently been made compulsory for time deposits of more than two years maturity. There, however, indexing proper still competes with what is sometimes called "pre-indexing," that is, the promise of a total remuneration, comprising both interest and "monetary correction," set in advance. Indexing is not applied to sight deposits (or to cash). Most commercial bank, as well as finance company and investment bank, loans are sufficiently short-term to be made at pre-indexed rates.

Finally, it should be mentioned that new ordinary life insurance policies, as well as so-called endowment policies, are indexed. The companies, in turn, protect themselves by investing in indexed securities, indexed mortgages, or equities and real estate.

The Tax System. One of the most important applications of indexing is to direct taxes and to tax debts. For some years before 1964, the progressive rate schedule of Brazil's personal income tax was adjusted in accordance with periodic changes in minimum wages. Since 1964, the schedule has been adjusted annually at least in rough proportion to the cost-of-living index, but greater adjustments have been made at times to favor the lower brackets.

The most radical change in the tax system involved the corporate income tax. Even before 1964 the periodic writing up of fixed assets had been permitted. However, the writing up served purely cosmetic purposes because it was not allowed to affect depreciation allowances. Under the system introduced after 1964, depreciation allowances deductible from profits are based on the adjusted value (according to the wholesale price index) of fixed assets and, in addition, considerable scope exists for accelerated depreciation. Later on, the final logical step was taken by permitting the deduction from profits of the adjustments necessary to maintain the real value of working capital. Like indexing of the progressive personal income tax schedule of rates, indexing of depreciation allowances and inventory adjustments made tax rates reasonable for the first time in many years and no longer confiscatory of purely illusory profits.

Logically, the increase in value of credit instruments corresponding to indexing is not taxable to the individual creditor (nor to the corporate creditor insofar as this is necessary to maintain his owned working capital intact) and is, like interest, a tax-deductible expense to the debtor.

Last, but not least, it should be mentioned that indexing is also applied to tax debts of all kinds. This provision eliminated the earlier incentive to delay payments since the interest rate chargeable on delays was low.

Controlled Prices. Indexing also made easier the adjustment, in line with inflation, of rates and rents (there had been a far-reaching decontrol of prices in general in 1964). For the most part, rates in Brazil are set so as to produce net earnings equal to a stated percentage of the utility's total assets; these earnings defray all capital costs. Despite some earlier provisions to mitigate the effect of inflation, it was only after 1964 that the authorities permitted public utilities not only to write up their assets periodically but also to make corresponding increases in rates, so as to produce the permissible rate of return in real terms. The general acceptance of indexing also made it easier in practice to adjust upwards the prices charged by government enterprises, even outside the utility field.

Inflation combined with rent control and usury laws had destroyed the market for rental housing and also had greatly reduced the availability of housing finance. Even before 1964, indexed rent contracts had been permitted in certain cases. However, it was only as a result of applying indexing to housing finance that a very large increase in building activity for owner-occupied, as well as rental, housing became possible. Mortgage contracts are indexed on wholesale prices but in the case of low-income housing, where the interest rate is also subsidized, contracts can be indexed on the minimum wage. In this case an equalizaton fund in the National Housing Bank is designed to absorb any difference between payments due from debtors and those due to lenders which may result from any difference in the movement of the indexes (since the obtention of housing finance is indexed on wholesale prices). Similarly, along with wholesale prices, the minimum wage is still used for the indexing of certain rent contracts (most rent contracts are free of any control).

Exchange Rates. For a period of several years (1964 to 1968), the exchange rate was adjusted infrequently in large steps, which discouraged exports by causing uncertainty and which generally led to large disturbing capital flows just before an expected change and just after a change had occurred. Since 1968, a system of small adjustments in the exchange rate at irregular intervals of between ten days and two months has been in effect. The predominant influence in these adjustments has been the differential between Brazil's inflation and the rate of inflation prevailing in its main trading partners.

Highlights of the Brazilian Economy since 1964

In early 1964, the annual rate of inflation in Brazil was over 100 percent, whereas in 1972, after an almost unbroken decreasing trend for several years, the wholesale price index rose just 16 percent, and the same rate of increase was registered in 1973. As a result both of the worldwide acceleration of inflation and particularly the abolition in March and April of most price controls and subsidies (which had been intensified in 1973), prices rose at a more rapid rate in the first five months of 1974, but the increase has been much lower beginning with June 1974, and inflation is expected to resume its gradual annual decline. Before 1964, real GNP growth in Brazil was irregular although, on average, not low. Since the end of 1967, however, it has been running at rates which have never been less than 9 percent, have averaged in excess of 10 percent—a much higher rate than ever before—and in 1973 reached over 11 percent.

Until 1964 the infrastructure of the economy grew at a relatively slow rate and exports lagged. The resulting bottlenecks and recurrent balance-of-payments crises held down the general growth rate of the economy. Since 1964, there has been a radical change. Rapid growth has occurred in the generation of electricity, in communications, in transportation, and in other aspects of the social as well as economic infrastructure. There has been an enormous development of housing construction including low-cost housing. Exports have grown spectacularly in volume as well as value.

Real minimum wages fell until 1968, as already mentioned, but in more recent years they have remained approximately stable and, as already noted, have been relevant to a declining proportion of the labor force. Also, average real wages have increased annually at something like 3 or 4 percent and, most recently, more in many sectors and regions. The guidelines do not prevent larger wage increases either for individual or for groups of workers as long as productivity increases make them possible without unreasonable price increases, which would be disallowed by the price supervision machinery. The average real wage increases mentioned are less than the growth rate of the economy per head of population and the difference reflects a choice—a highly successful choice—in favor of more rapid elimination of unemployment and underemployment.

To measure economic welfare, government services rendered to the population (often gratuitously) must be added to real wages. These services include greatly increased expenditures (in relation to GNP) on education, on health, and on low-cost housing (which is subsidized); they also include the institution of schemes for non-contributory endowment policies for employees established on the basis of employers' contributions offset by federal tax reductions (Social Integration Program). The benefits derived from these services are, of course, inversely proportional to real income levels.

Some Tentative Conclusions

The Effects of Indexing in Brazil. The performance of the Brazilian economy since 1964 has sometimes been described as an "economic miracle." Without indexing, it would have been impossible for the sharp reduction in the rate of inflation to have been achieved simultaneously with a remarkable upsurge in growth. But indexing was not a sufficient condition for success, either in reducing inflation or in stimulating growth.

1. The relationship between indexing and the reduction in the rate of inflation is a complex one. Indexing avoids the textbook effects of inflation: inequities in income distribution (in modern conditions, among categories of wage earners rather than between them and other economic groups), distortion of the productive and financial structures and destruction of the incentive to save. But indexing creates feedback effects from yesterday's inflation to today's: the greater the number of sectors that are shielded from the the effects of inflation, the less can the economy neutralize inflationary impulses.

Nevertheless, indexing can help indirectly even in reducing the rate of inflation gradually. By offering protection against the effects of inflation, indexing makes it possible to live with inflation and, therefore, to avoid attempts to end inflation by shock treatment. Whenever the rate of inflation is substantial, policies aimed at its rapid termination appear to fail (except under fairly peculiar circumstances) and the failure then discourages further attempts to curb inflation. By institutionalizing protection against inflation on a nondiscriminatory basis, indexing may also discourage excessive claims for income and price increases in anticipation of inflation, thereby making easier the reduction of the rate of inflation without recession. The avoidance of the textbook effects of inflation may itself have anti-inflationary virtue. Sectoral bottlenecks in production and insufficient savings had been powerful factors in Brazil since the early fifties in forcing the government and the monetary authorities, respectively, to intervene to supply deficiencies, almost unavoidably with inflationary effects.

In Brazil, the new wage formula was certainly essential in making it possible to reduce the rate of inflation. But the virtue of the new wage formula was not the introduction of indexing but rather the replacement of a sometimes haphazard, and at best less rational, method of indexing wages by a more rational one.

2. It is obvious that, for growth to accelerate, it was essential for Brazil to avoid, through indexing, the textbook effects of inflation—that is, the distortions which caused bottlenecks, including those affecting the financial sector of the economy. In view of the important role which had to be assumed in the Brazilian development process by the public sector, indexing was also helpful to that sector

because it rationalized the tax system and particularly because it enabled the government to borrow from the market and helped government enterprises to maintain their profitability.

3. There are other factors besides indexing which have been crucial to Brazil's economic success.

Indexing—as we have seen—directly reduces the ability of the economy to absorb the inflationary impulses emanating from given sectors or income categories at the expense of other sectors or categories. The rate of inflation could become explosive, therefore, unless anti-inflationary policies are followed in all other respects. This means that an incomes policy—which will attempt to protect real wages only to the point that their growth is compatible with the country's productivity increase and its employment objectives—is required. In the presence of widespread oligopoly it also means price guidelines for the oligopolistic sectors as an important ingredient of the anti-inflationary strategy. Furthermore, it means demand management that will validate this price and incomes policy—neither more nor less. While this basic requirement of demand management was observed as a general rule, monetary policy had a distinct bias towards avoiding liquidity crises so that demand management, insofar as it did err, did not do so on the side of restraint. This fact made the use of price and wage guidelines indispensable to the anti-inflationary strategy, whatever might have been the case otherwise.

In demand management, improved tax administration and expenditure control played an essential role in reducing the cash budget deficit from a high proportion of GNP to a negligible one. Equally important has been the control over internal and, later, when capital inflows from abroad became important, external credit. Control over internal credit has been very largely a matter of institution building, including the establishment of the Central Bank and the National Housing Bank, the development of new types of private financial institutions, the Social Integration Program, and so on. The development of new credit instruments has also been important; they include, in addition to the indexed varieties already mentioned, short-term, nonindexed Treasury bills used for open market operations by the Central Bank. Controls on external credit would have been impossible without the application of indexing to the exchange rate—in small steps at frequent but unpredictable intervals. These adjustments eliminated speculative inflows and outflows of capital, while at the same time stimulating long-term lending to Brazil, because they gave assurance that the balance of payments would remain viable.

With respect to economic growth, an essential part of the success story has been increasing confidence and cooperation between the government and the private sector. Institution-building has already been mentioned in connection with the successful growth performance. So is the improvement of the tax and expenditure control systems. Important changes in tax laws have gone far beyond the introduction of indexing—important as this has been to prevent the destruction by inflation of the incentive to save, indeed, of the very possibility of saving. They include a far-reaching system of tax incentives designed to stimulate saving by stimulating investment in marketable securities and other financial instruments, as well as tax incentives (including tariff exemptions) designed to promote investment in real assets in certain sectors and regions of the country. Also important has been the development of labor law, which gave workers the choice between (1) certain indemnities in case of unjust dismissal and (2) participation in a noncontributory fund (distinct from that established under the Social Integration Program) which they would receive upon retirement, disability, or unemployment or could withdraw for specified purposes such as the purchase or construction of a house. The latter option, which tends to enhance labor mobility and productivity, was adopted by an overwhelming proportion of workers.

Some General Reflections on Indexing. In many countries the adoption of widespread indexing, though an important change in the economic system, would require no change in the law. In others it would merely require reestablishing freedom of contract or changing the manner in which this freedom is restricted. The most complicated changes would probably be those which would have to be made in the tax laws and in the laws governing public sector activities in general. The Brazilian experience also shows that it would be naive to believe that a generalized system of indexing can be installed and then left to its own devices, that is, that rules can take over from authorities in this respect. Indexing means that certain magnitudes are indexed on others and this implies either lags or reliance on estimates rather than past events. Both lags and estimates can result in highly bothersome and misleading signals. Besides the possibility of price repression there is thus a possibility that in the attempt to avoid false signals the formula by which past events affect the magnitudes to be indexed will be changed or estimates made which will avoid what seemed to be false signals. Nevertheless, the adoption under appropriate conditions of a generalized system of indexing, even where it is not in retrospect revealed to have been perfect or even simply automatic at all times, will certainly be found to have prevented major distortions which would otherwise arise under inflation.

Indexing is a way of living with inflation which makes inflation less harmful than it would otherwise be. But price stability is still better than inflation—even indexed inflation, which may, on balance, delay progress in reducing the rate of inflation. Whether the advantages of indexing outweigh the disadvantages depends particularly on the strength of the underlying factors which keep inflation going and the state of expectations.

One important aspect of indexing should be obvious. Just as the absence of indexing under inflation may lead to distortions, so may partial indexing—and the distortions caused by partial indexing may even be the worse of the two kinds. Like partial indexing, the indexing of competing items on quite divergent indices can cause distortions, unless these are prevented by offsetting incentives and disincentives of other kinds.

A somewhat similar problem arises where relatively long-term loans (like mortgages) have been financed by financial institutions on the basis of unindexed, relatively short-term borrowings (like savings deposits). This latter problem means that a country which, unlike Brazil, had a considerable volume of such loans and deposits before the introduction of indexing would be facing a very difficult problem on introducing indexing. The problem is not insoluble, however, and is in principle no different from the problem which arises when nominal interest rates rise for prolonged periods.

It should be clear from the Brazilian experience that indexing by itself is not a way either to combat inflation or to stimulate growth. It was certainly never seen in Brazil as a policy which could be used by itself, permitting policy makers to dispense with vigorous anti-inflation and growth measures.